Finance
for Growth

Mergers, Acquisitions and Alternative Corporate Strategies
Hill Samuel Bank Limited

Tax: Strategic Corporate Tax Planning
Price Waterhouse

Finance for Growth
National Westminster Bank PLC

Company Law and Competition
S J Berwin & Co

Marketing: Communicating with the Consumer
D'Arcy Masius Benton & Bowles

Information Technology: The Catalyst for Change
PA Consulting Group

Marketing to the Public Sector and Industry
Rank Xerox Limited

Transport and Distribution
TNT Express

Property
Edward Erdman

Employment and Training
Manpower plc .

Audio cassette documentaries are available on each of the titles above, showing through case studies, and interviews with senior executives, how British companies can take advantage of new markets in Europe. The cassettes are available at £9.95 through bookshops or from Didasko Ltd, Didasko House, Wennington, Huntingdon, Cambs PE17 2LX.

Finance
for Growth
National Westminster Bank PLC

With a Foreword by Kenneth Warren, MP
Chairman of the Trade and Industry Select Committee

Published in association with
CBI Initiative 1992

MERCURY BOOKS
Published by Gold Arrow Publications Limited

First published in 1989
by Mercury Books
Reprinted 1989, 1990
by Mercury Books
Gold Arrow Publications Limited, 862 Garratt Lane, London SW17 0NB

Set in Plantin by Phoenix Photosetting, Chatham
Printed and bound in Great Britain by
Butler & Tanner Ltd, Frome, Somerset

British Library Cataloguing in Publication Data

Finance for growth
   1. Financial services
   I. National Westminster Bank
   II. Confederation of British Industry
   332.1

  ISBN 1-85251-022-6

Contents

Foreword   vii

Preface   ix

1. Introduction   1
2. The impact of the single market on the financial sector   7
3. Delivery systems, payment methods and advanced electronic systems   29
4. Short-term trade-related bank facilities   37
5. Alternative short-term borrowing techniques   61
6. Medium- and long-term borrowing   65
7. Interest-rate risk management   75
8. Currency exposure management   85
9. Currency and interest-rate swaps   89
10. Limited recourse finance   91
11. Leasing   95
12. Franchising   99
13. Sources of EC finance   103
14. Raising capital funds   111
15. Case studies   123

Appendix 1: Banking systems in the EC   133

Appendix 2: Legislative impact on banks and the financial
                sector   143

Appendix 3: Contact addresses   157

Bibliography   159

Glossary   161

Index   169

Foreword

Financial services trading worldwide hinges on three dominant centres: Tokyo, New York and London. On our own capital city rests the future strength of the EEC as a financial force in the world. Success is the hallmark of the City. Its credit rating in the eyes of the world is 'Triple A'.

UK financial services bring to our nation a trading surplus of £9 billion a year, an invaluable asset for a nation with a growing adverse gap in visibles. This welcome feat is equivalent to the three principal visible imports added together: German cars, information technology equipment and paper. Our quality of business is seen from abroad as rising, thus reinforcing the attraction of doing business in Britain. The Financial Services Act and the regulation of financial business standards in the UK is working, but experience is demonstrating it requires self-regulation of its costs to ensure the competitiveness of those regulated is not eroded.

1992 has already started to arrive. Many key features will be operational before 1 January 1993, but others may not be installed before the millenium. Although the targets of free trade across frontiers are well defined, many member states have substantial internal legislative tasks to complete before the single market can exist. It is clear, however, that each sovereign state is determined to achieve free trade with all the others, so wise companies are tuning their strategies to seek new business opportunities and plan appropriate financial resources before each hurdle is formally removed.

With so much at stake I strongly counsel business leaders to learn exactly what 1992 means for their enterprises. They must be able to pass with distinction every question on the Treaty of Rome, the Single European Act, the effect of presidencies on 1992 and above all, who's who in the corridors of power of the European Economic Community. Homework may be a nightmare, but business prosperity and survival rests on market knowledge.

The Japanese are constantly probing the meaning of 1992 as a chance to follow on from their domination of world consumer goods into becoming the power base of world finance. The United States is reacting from a slow start caused by its first vision of 1992 as 'Fortress

Europe'. Nothing in the world of business and finance is ever static, but we in the UK are ahead and must keep ahead in the dash to the new markets.

The assets of the big banks in France and Germany may exceed our own, but our financial institutions' worldwide expertise exceeds, in my opinion, all the rest of the EEC put together. This is not to deny the huge economic success of West German enterprise, but UK institutions clearly see the whole world as their market and rightly so. The EEC will only reap the benefits of 1992 when its member states, the Council of Ministers, the Commissioners and every Tom, Jean and Horst in business boardrooms have the vision to understand that free trade around the world is the true target.

Kenneth R. Warren, MP
Chairman of the Trade and Industry Select Committee

Preface

CBI Initiative 1992 is vitally important to UK business and NatWest is delighted to be part of it. The aim of *Finance for Growth* is to explain how companies can finance their European strategies – whether they are boosting exports or completely refocusing their approach to Europe.

As freer markets emerge, the part to be played by bankers will be crucial if UK businesses are to capitalise at this time of evolution. At NatWest, we are ideally placed to help UK companies. We are no strangers to Europe and have had representation there for more than seventy years. We now have a presence in ten of the twelve member states of the Community.

As a leading European bank, we have an extensive range of trade-related financial services, loans and capital funding products. We also provide advice and market intelligence on economic and industrial conditions so vital to business.

Our approach to Europe is straightforward – to concentrate on the things we do well. That means expanding the range and availability of the financial services we provide for both personal and corporate customers in the Community. We are building businesses that make sense locally . . . to French customers in France, to Spanish customers in Spain.

But one of our key business objectives is to help our UK corporate customers – from the smallest firm to the biggest international corporation. Our contribution to CBI Initiative 1992 is a major step in our pursuit of this aim.

We have concentrated on practical issues in this book. We have been helped considerably by the case studies, and I would like to thank the companies involved for their contribution. I would also like to thank the book's editor, Michael Imeson, for his help in co-ordinating the publication of *Finance for Growth*. I trust readers will find this book a useful guide to the many opportunities the single European market has to offer.

Lord Alexander of Weedon
Chairman, National Westminster Bank PLC

1. Introduction

Much is being made of the dismantling of trade barriers within the EC, as enshrined in the Single European Act. The optimists say the creation of a single market by the end of 1992 of around 323 million people will make the Community's companies more efficient, allow the EC to compete better against the unified economic powers of the USA and Japan and make us all, in the end, more prosperous.

Pessimists, however, believe that the barriers will take far longer to dismantle than planned, and in certain cases may not come down fully at all. Some member states, the UK included, are resistant to the current proposals for fiscal harmonisation, and although most areas of the single market proposals are subject to qualified majority voting at the Council of Ministers, fiscal matters require unanimity. There are wider political problems too, since member states may be unwilling to surrender their sovereignty over a range of domestic policy issues.

Yet amid the fuss, and the claims and counter claims, it is important to bear in mind what the Common Market has already achieved in developing trade between member states and fostering economic and political co-operation. When the UK, for example, joined the EC in 1973, exports to the other eleven states, which now make up the Community, accounted for 35 per cent of the UK's total. This has steadily risen and for the first nine months of 1988 the figure stood at 50 per cent. Imports from member states accounted for 38 per cent of the total in 1973; by 1988 they accounted for 53 per cent. This is a considerable increase, especially considering the UK's Commonwealth heritage and its traditionally diverse world trade.

1992 is bound to accelerate that trend, despite what the pessimists say, and cause at the same time industrial and commercial structures to change. The costs to business of adjusting to these changes will be high. The key to success will be to develop a sound business strategy, whether it is aimed at exploiting the Continental market or protecting the domestic one. Companies will need to take a pragmatic approach to developing their strategies, looking closely at matters such as marketing, sales, distribution, production, product development, purchasing, joint ventures and acquisitions, and then at how they are going to finance it all.

Cash flow

Open account

EDI

Effective financial management is crucial if business strategies are to be successful, and this is where banks and other financial advisers, with their services, funding and advice, come into the picture. The main aim of this book is to look in detail at the finance available to companies that want to take advantage of the opportunities and combat the threats created by the single market.* Businesses will have to consider the short-term and long-term implications for their cash flow and balance sheet. Cash flow may be affected by changes in their terms of trade forced upon them by a need to match terms offered by competitors in their own backyards; and in the short term they may need to look at capital expenditure to gear up to the new demands. For instance, the removal of frontier controls within the EC will make it more difficult to control the movement of goods once they have left the vendor. This is likely to lead to even more trading on open account than there is now, which in turn will fuel demand for factoring, credit reference and other banking services which can provide finance and minimise trade risk. Chapter 4 looks at this in more detail.

The international movement of payments (Chapter 3) is becoming much more efficient, and no doubt more companies will eschew paper-based systems of transferring money (such as bank drafts) and opt instead for corporate cash management services, where the company is linked electronically to the bank. The subscribing company has a computer terminal in its office, linked to the bank's computer by telephone line and through this many services can be offered including money transfer.

A further development relevant to electronic banking services is Electronic Data Interchange (EDI), or 'paperless trading' (Chapter 3). Many companies, especially the multinationals, are developing EDI as a means of transmitting orders, invoices and other documentation between traders' computers, thus saving time over traditional paper-moving methods. The banks are getting involved, and it is now becoming possible for documentary letters of credit to be transmitted from a bank to an exporter. Some banks are even considering providing EDI networks. In the future, companies which do not belong to EDI systems will risk losing orders or being paid more slowly.

Other areas which businesses must examine in the light of the single market are in the provision of various short-term methods of trade finance, such as documentary credits, bills of exchange and factoring services (Chapter 4); alternative short-term borrowing techniques (Chapter 5); medium- and long-term borrowing (Chapter 6); interest-rate risk management and currency exposure management (Chapters 7, 8 and 9); limited recourse finance (Chapter 10); franchising (Chapter 12); information on sources of EC finance and EC-funded

* This book was compiled with information current, in general, at 31 March 1989.

projects (Chapter 13); and the provision of local financing and banking arrangements abroad (Appendix 1).

Terms of trade

Greater competition at home, meanwhile, may force manufacturers to relax their terms of trade, by lengthening credit periods to customers from thirty days, say, to sixty days, or by shortening delivery periods. If this happens, cash flow will be affected and suppliers might need to increase their overdraft facilities, for which they would almost certainly turn to their bank.

On the capital investment front, there is likely to be a trend towards larger units of production in one country, with these units delivering across borders to other member states. That will create a need not only

Capital finance

for capital finance (Chapter 14) – to build those units, to buy new equipment, and to build distribution centres – but may also necessitate new methods of collecting debts from several countries in different currencies. Off-balance-sheet finance, such as leasing (Chapter 11), will also be required. The harmonisation of technical and safety standards by 1992 could prove expensive for companies and provoke substantial capital investment.

Corporate alliances

Some companies will consider joint ventures as a means of increasing their penetration of EC markets, and of protecting and increasing their UK market share. One example of this is Italy's Fiat, which is seeking 'commercial alliances' – not mergers – with US or European car makers in the run up to 1992. The investment banks and the investment banking arms of the big clearers are an essential port of call for funding and advice on joint ventures, venture capital, mergers and acquisitions and other investment opportunities (Chapter 14). Cross-border takeover activity has already started to hot up. A single market will lead to more takeovers as companies either seek ready-made access to other markets, or restructure and rationalise in order to gain economies of scale. At the same time, mergers, share-swaps, poison pills, leveraged buy-outs and other bid paraphernalia will be used as defences against predators. Chapter 15, a series of case studies illustrating various forms of finance, includes some real-life examples of acquisition finance.

UK firms are at the forefront of European acquisitions activity, which almost doubled in 1988. According to a leading corporate finance adviser, in the first seven months of 1988 there were 128 takeovers by UK companies in Europe valued at £1.3 billion, compared with 134 takeovers worth £1.25 billion for the whole of 1987. However, these figures fall a long way short of UK acquisitions in the USA, of which there were 314 worth $29.2 billion in 1987, and 335 worth $20.6 billion in the first nine months of 1988.

At the same time, there are worries that the UK is becoming the first port of call for takeovers because its securities markets are the biggest in the EC and they provide a hospitable environment for predators to launch hostile takeovers. This has led to calls for the tightening up of takeover rules, such as a lowering of the 30 per cent trigger point for bids. It has also prompted demands for the creation of a 'level playing-field'. Siemens, for instance, is immune from hostile takeover because of its intricate share structure and powerful block of equity held by Deutsche Bank.

Information

As they go about their business researching the single market, companies might find useful the economic and market intelligence departments that most UK commercial banks have. These can supply corporate customers with up-to-date information on the economies of all the member states and on sales opportunities in specific industrial sectors; and they are a good source of information on the Commission's economic policies and funding programmes. The banks' intelligence departments also provide statistics and analyses on exchange rates and interest rates.

Banking in the EC

How will bank services to corporate customers change in the lead up to 1992? Whatever a company's financial requirements are, or will be, in the EC, it should find that UK banking services are already more than adequate for their needs. Financial products are unlikely to change much in the next few years. What *is* likely to change is how these products are delivered in the Community. Not content to rest on their laurels and mindful of the increased competition in financial services, the banks are planning improvements that will be tailored to the new economic conditions.

One of the biggest areas of development will be in electronic banking and EDI. As trade volumes increase in the EC, payments systems will be speeded up. Slow, paper-based money transfers will give way to greater use of fast electronic delivery systems such as SWIFT (Society for Worldwide Interbank Financial Telecommunications) and CHAPS (Clearing House Automated Payments System). Banks are also working on EDI systems, as mentioned earlier, whereby companies will be able to link up with the banks' computers, and with other companies' computers, to exchange trading information and possibly transfer money.

The other noticeable areas of change are the planned expansions in the banks' European branch networks. The leading UK clearing banks aim to increase their representation either by acquiring banks in the EC or, as is more likely, entering into joint venture agreements with them. To build up a network from scratch would be very expensive. The major banks from other member states will also be seeking to expand. Although much has been said about some banks having pan-European objectives, they are unlikely to be achieved in the foreseeable future because of the high capital costs involved. Banks are looking for increased representation in the EC for three reasons:

one, to service the needs of their UK corporate customers who are also expanding in Europe; two, to find new corporate and personal customers abroad and make the most of the liberalisation of the financial markets; and three, to protect their existing customer base.

The Second Banking Directive aims to harmonise banking in the EC through the Single Banking Licence, which allows banks to provide throughout the Community the sorts of financial services they can provide in their own countries. They will be subject to home country control, with only minimal interference from host country regulations. Cultural and language barriers will still exist, of course, and these will be a challenge to surmount.

Financial differences

UK banks believe that efficient, low cost services developed in the liberalised environment of the UK, and which have stood the test of foreign competiton, will find a ready market in the EC, which has in the past been more protected. At the moment, banking operations, market structures and regulatory frameworks vary greatly from member state to member state, and this has a bearing on the types and price of services banks in each member state can offer. For example, because France has exchange controls, residents are still generally not allowed to have bank accounts abroad or to open foreign currency accounts in France. French banks are also restricted on the amounts they can lend to non-residents. In France, unlike the situation in the UK, overdrafts and short-term loans are not used that frequently as short-term trade finance – the discount of trade paper is more popular. By contrast, in West Germany overdrafts are the most common form of short-term financing, but they are comparatively expensive. (For more details on member states' banking systems and practices see Appendix 1.)

Differences such as these are likely to disappear over time as the banking market becomes more unified and as more banks merge or create partnerships. This kind of activity has been much in evidence: the Royal Bank of Scotland recently went into partnership with Banco Santander in Spain; Belgium's Générale Bank and the Netherlands' AMRO Bank have taken a 5 per cent share stake in each other; other partnerships to date include Banco de Bilbao and Banco de Vizcaya in Spain; and in West Germany there have been talks between Westdeutsche Landesbank and Hessische Landesbank. Deutsche Bank is the prime example of aggressive expansion. It has acquired Banca d'America & d'Italia, bought out partners in a Portuguese merchant bank, taken a 50 per cent stake in H. Alfred de Bary (a Dutch investment bank) and increased its holding in Banco Comercial Transatlantico in Spain.

Deutsche Bank

A handful of West German banks are being partially privatised, but the sale of all state business has been blocked in France by the Mitterrand government and this has brought to a halt the proposal for a

10 per cent equity stake exchange between Crédit Lyonnais and Commerzbank. In West Germany, few of the privately owned banks have shares quoted on the stock exchange and the existing structure of family and friendly shareholdings will protect them from predators; co-operative takeovers appear to be the only realistic route.

These developments are just the tip of the iceberg, and the next few years are likely to see a major change in the European banking map. There are about 14,000 banks in Europe, so the market is highly fragmented. Progress towards mergers and acquisitions is likely to be impeded because many countries have a rigid structure separating commercial, savings, mortgage, co-operative and investment banking, and cross-border groupings will not be easy as many banks are owned by governments or communities which will be loath to see ownership go outside that state.

Before going on to look at the various forms of finance available to companies preparing for 1992, the next chapter describes in detail the impact of 1992 on the financial services sector itself.

The twelve member states								
1987	Area (000 sq mls)	Pop. (million)	Population growth (% p.a. 1977–87)	GDP (£bn)	GDP per cap. (£)	Distribution of GDP (% 1987)		
						Agric.	Ind.	Services
Belgium	11.8	9.9	0.0	85	8,586	2*	32*	66*
Denmark	16.6	5.1	0.1	62	12,157	5*	24*	71*
France	212.9	55.6	0.5	533	9,586	4	38	58
Greece	51.0	10.0	0.7	29	2,900	14*	30*	56*
Italy	116.3	57.3	0.3	457	7,975	4	34	62
Luxembourg	1.0	0.4	0.2	3.8	9,500	n.a.	n.a.	n.a.
Netherlands	13.1	14.7	0.5	131	8,912	4	33	63
Portugal	35.8	10.2	0.5	22	2,157	9†	40†	51†
Republic of Ireland	26.6	3.6	0.9	18	5,000	11†	25†	64†
Spain	196.6	38.7	0.7	175	4,522	7†	35†	58†
UK	94.2	56.8	0.1	403	7,095	2	37	61
West Germany	96.9	61.1	0.0	683	11,178	2	42	56
Total	872.8	323.4	0.3	2,602	8,045	–	–	–

† 1985
* 1986

2. The impact of the single market on the financial sector

Progress

In the field of banking and related financial services much progress has already been made towards the single market. The First Banking Directive (1977), which created the basic right of credit institutions to establish in all member states and laid down the minimum legal requirements, was a significant step on the road to a single barrier-free market in financial services. This will be followed by the Second Banking Directive and other directives which will establish the minimum harmonisation of supervisory standards necessary to entitle a credit institution authorised in one member state to provide core banking services throughout the Community, either through a branch or on a services basis, without further authorisation in any other member state.

Obstacles

Nevertheless, at present there are still considerable hindrances to the completion of a single market. The EC aims to remove many of them, although other obstacles, notably on questions of a single currency and a European central bank, remain. There are those who argue that the creation of a European Central Bank is not feasible until there is in place a unified exchange-rate regime. But objections to these ideas are usually more basic because they are seen as cutting at the very roots of sovereignty – a currency is inextricably intertwined with complex and emotional concepts of national identity.

Sovereignty

Withholding tax

Sovereignty will also be at issue with the freeing up of capital flows within the Community. For while this is critical to the creation of a unified market place, it has implications for tax harmonisation and interest-rate strategies. For example, the Commission has drafted a proposal on the divisive issue of withholding tax. It says that the way to harmonise this is to tax bank interest and investments at source. For some this amounts to a choice between changing the bank secrecy laws in their respective countries or bringing in a withholding tax applicable to all twelve member states.

Luxembourg and the UK have substantial although different objections to harmonising withholding tax. The UK does not want it and in Luxembourg there is an aversion to creating a tax evasion problem that does not exist at the moment. (The West Germans learnt that lesson to their cost: when they announced a 10 per cent withholding tax on domestic bonds to take effect from January 1989, an estimated DM20 billion ($10.7 billion) fled West Germany into Luxembourg in the first seven months of 1988. The proposal has since been dropped.) Bankers and officials in Luxembourg get distinctly frosty if you refer to Luxembourg as a 'tax haven', but there are queues of banks waiting to move inside its tax-agreeable borders; a withholding tax would quickly reduce those numbers. France, on the other hand, is said to have a rather inefficient tax collection system. It levies a steep 25 per cent on deposits and is loath to create a situation which will result in a substantial flight of capital. But as a *quid pro quo* for agreeing to the free movement of capital, France is demanding protection.

There is an additional problem because harmonisation alone, even if achievable, will not solve anything unless the withholding tax is less than 10 per cent. If it is any higher, funds may be attracted to Switzerland, the Channel Islands or even Liechtenstein. However, there is now an inexorable move towards a unified market place. This momentum has been given added impetus by new decision-making procedures, such as qualified majority voting on a number of issues.

Nevertheless, more and more governments and their bureaucracies are succumbing not just to the force of the market place but to its wiles and ever-innovative ways of bridging the gap between those who have the money and those who want to borrow it.

The gradual approach

There has also been within the Commission and member state governments a growing acceptance of the need for a gradual approach. One important lesson has been learnt and that is the impracticality of trying to achieve total harmonisation. It is this acceptance that has led to the compromise concepts of 'mutual recognition' and 'home

Home country control

country control'. Home country control underlies the whole 1992 financial programme. According to this principle, enshrined in the Second Banking Directive, a bank or credit institution allowed by its own regulatory authority to perform at home any of the core banking activities will be allowed to do the same throughout the Community without having to establish in each member state. However, regulatory authorities such as the Bank of England could be concerned about the possible repercussions of such principles, which might encourage banks to establish themselves in member states with the lowest supervisory standards and trade throughout the Community from this base.

The question remains whether home country control and mutual recognition are able to provide a legal framework for a unified internal market. The Community's Banking Federation would like to see more harmonisation of individual banking regimes. For those who believe mutual recognition is the best way to combine deregulation and liberalisation with effective consumer protection, there remains the difficult problem of setting the right balance between home and host country control.

Own funds

The Community has moved towards a common position on minimum capital standards or own funds for banks but differences remain on questions of revaluation reserves. Some of the non-G10 Community members (Denmark, Greece, Portugal, the Republic of Ireland, Spain) were not party to the Basel Committee proposals on capital requirements. However, there is a long way to go before the Community agrees to a common position on capital adequacy for financial services. The UK's approach of matching capital flexibly with 'position' risks is not liked in Continental Europe, which largely prefers a single lump sum against all eventualities. The Commission has to get round the accusations that the first approach could involve over-regulation while the second could involve excessive capitalisation.

The Community has also yet to address the problem of taxing monetary assets such as demand deposits, because in some countries they are treated as instruments of monetary policy. They do not want a tax driving a wedge between deposit and loan rates. But few doubt that sooner or later the bullet will have to be bitten because if the Community goal of bank integration is even partially achieved, deposit and loan business will simply move across borders to banks offering the best rates.

All this shows that while substantial progress has been made, there is still a long way to go. Of some 300 legislative proposals set out in the White Paper only 47 per cent of them had been accepted by the end of 1988 and those have been the relatively non-contentious ones. Of the balance, around 10 per cent have made little or no progress at all and have yet to be drafted.

For business in the Community the impact of 1992 on the financial services sector will mean greater availability of a wider variety of services and products. In the opinion of what is now known as the Cecchini Report, *1992: The Benefits of a Single Market*, it could also result in considerably reduced costs (bank charges and commissions, for example). However, the conclusions of the Cecchini Report are at best guesstimates and the Community as a whole will have to wait for the full impact to filter through. The most important element here will be the implementation of the competition laws to ensure a truly free and competitive market place.

Cost of financial services

According to a report prepared by Price Waterhouse for the Cecchini Report, there are considerable differences in the pricing of financial services throughout the Community. For example, at the time of the report, bank loans to consumers in the UK carried more than three times the margin over the money-market rate than they did in Belgium. The West German and French rates were equally high. Yet mortgages in France and West Germany had a margin twice that of rates for mortgages in the UK.

The Cecchini Report takes an upbeat approach. On the optimistic side, it has been estimated that with full implementation of the 1992 proposals consumer prices throughout the Community could fall by 6 per cent after six years and raise real GDP by 4.5 per cent. One effect of this, the Commission believes, will be the creation of two million new jobs.

But even the most starry-eyed advocate of a single market knows that any inclination towards the creation of 'Fortress Europe' would stir retaliation from other major world economies. The USA is already deeply suspicious of some of the trends and is keeping a weather eye open for the slightest sign of protectionism.

Reciprocity
Article 7 of the Second Banking Directive addresses the issue of 'reciprocity': a similar clause is planned for the Investment Services Directive. There are those who have interpreted reciprocity very narrowly, arguing for national non-discriminatory treatment for their own companies operating abroad. In other words, they want to be treated exactly as if they were a local company. Then there is the broader approach which says Community banks should be accorded the same rights in non-Community states as non-Community banks have within the Community. Such a definition would oblige the US and Japanese authorities to give powers to their own banks as wide as those intended to be given to banks in the Community. This would require major legislative changes in both countries, something that has hitherto proved more than vexatious.

Such an approach could also force countries such as the UK or France to refuse entry to a new Japanese institution because Portugal or Greece, perhaps, felt they were not getting a fair crack of the whip in Tokyo.

Whatever interpretation might be given to the issue of 'reciprocity', the UK found the original proposals unacceptable, believing that they would work against the principle of open financial markets. Consequently, the UK has proposed that the text of the clause should make clear that the objective is to achieve liberalisation of third country markets not to build protectionist barriers around the Community. Further, it is proposed that the 'reciprocity' powers shall be reserve powers, under tight political control, as opposed to being the subject of Community committee procedure.

One battle that does seem to have been won by Luxembourg and the UK is the apparent acceptance by the Commission of the notion that reciprocal rights should not be applied retroactively to non-

Community banks and credit organisations. This should also be the case with the Investment Services Directive.

Considering the complexity of what it is trying to achieve, the Commission's much-maligned officialdom has made great strides towards the goal of a single market. The Commission and the member states have not always seen eye to eye, but the progress towards 1992 has been and will continue to be a learning process for all for years to come.

The situation is, of course, constantly changing and it is important to keep abreast of developments through the Press and the relevant official sources as more legislation is agreed.

Appendix 2 goes into more detail on the legislation affecting banks and the financial sector at the time of writing. It covers the various banking directives, including the Second Banking Directive, which is the proposed foundation for banks and related credit institutions under the 1992 programme. It also looks at EC recommendations for the financial sector, which may eventually form the basis of directives. This includes recommendations on large exposures, deposit guarantees and electronic payments. Other legislation dealt with in Appendix 2 is that affecting securities, the liberalisation of capital movements, home/host country control and insurance.

Costs/benefits of banking legislation to UK business

Many of the measures being adopted by the Council of Ministers to create a single market in financial services do not directly concern the business community generally. But business is indirectly affected in so far as these measures govern the way banks conduct their affairs and provide protection for their customers. The purpose of the Second Banking Directive is to give banks the freedom to sell services to the consumer across the twelve member states but with adequate common supervision.

Business is more directly affected by legislation for the securities industry which lays down rules on:

- Stock exchange listings
- Prospectuses for public offers
- The publication of listed company reports
- The publication of share ownership changes
- Insider trading
- Securities transaction taxes

However, these laws are not designed to restrict but actually to facilitate a company's ability to raise capital on any Community exchange.

It is important for a company to read the Community legislation on the financial services industry alongside those Articles of the Treaty of Rome which aim to maximise competition and restrict any attempts at anti-competitive practices. For this to happen, every company, whether it is planning to move into Continental Europe or simply staying at home, must have at least one person fully conversant with what is and is not allowed under Community law. This includes a knowledge of what banks, merchant banks, brokerages and insurance companies may or may not offer or do. That person will need to be well versed in the opportunities and pitfalls afforded by legislation on:

- Banking and the movement of money around the Community

- Insurance for both individuals and corporates

- The securities industry

- Transport

- New technologies and the standardisation of equipment

- The movement of labour and professional staff, the recognition across borders of professional qualifications and training

Failure to keep abreast of these developments could mean loss of business opportunities and markets or, conversely, result in massive fines for being in breach of the Community's strict rules on anti-competitive practices.

There are more than 300 complex directives being planned which on the one hand will closely regulate the single market, and on the other will provide a framework for banking and business unfettered by borders and monopolistic or nationalistic practices. Cost apart, business cannot rely solely on the plethora of 'advisers' or 'consultants' to keep it informed. Nor can it expect Parliament to protect its back.

Anti-competitive practices

The point that must be remembered is that for the purposes of Articles 85 and 86 of the Treaty of Rome, which govern competition, financial services are included in the notion of 'trade'. The European Court has accepted that this is a concept that has 'wide scope'. This means that banks are not excluded from anti-competitive rules except where they are deemed to be performing services which are of 'general economic interest' under national legislation and which are not normal banking services.

Since 1986, after comprehensive research into commissions charged by banks throughout the Community, several anti-competitive practices have been abandoned, notably in Belgium, the Republic of Ireland and Italy. Nevertheless, the Commission has made some exceptions to its general policy of not allowing horizontal agreements for fixing prices and other trading conditions. For example, the Commission has agreed that charges to the customer for telephone bills, payment services and minimum charges for renting safes and for safe custody services do not affect trade between Community members and therefore do not contravene the competition laws of Article 85.

The message to business, as always, is to be vigilant because banking practices vary from member state to member state. Opening up the single market is not going to change that because the Community has accepted by majority vote the concepts of home/host country control and mutual recognition (see Appendix 2). Nevertheless, under the 1992 proposals, there are some general trends. In addition to limited exceptions for fixing prices, there are also exemptions allowable where it is necessary:

- To improve the interbank payment system

- To increase the supply of bank services to customers

- To expedite and speed up those services

It has been pointed out that these exceptions do not actually squash competition because agreements between banks on commissions do not directly affect the customer; the bank is at liberty not to pass on all or part of those charges.

There has been much speculation and some attempts at hard analysis to determine the possible reduction in financial services costs thought to be inevitable given the increased competition in a single market of 323 million people. The analysis and the source of the debate is the report prepared for the Commission by Paolo Cecchini, *1992: The Benefits of a Single Market*. The Cecchini Report acknowledges that there were considerable methodological difficulties in assessing the cost/benefit impact of the single market. It also accepts what it called the 'unevenness of the empirical data on European fragmentation'. But despite these problems, the Cecchini Report concludes that its analysis shows that the costs of a 'non-Europe' and, therefore, the potential gains exceed 200 billion ecu, or £140 billion. This figure is arrived at by attempting to chart the costs of border controls, customs red tape, divergent standards and technical regulations, conflicting business laws and protectionist procurement practices.

Potential gains in economic welfare for the EC resulting from completion of the internal market		
	billions ecu	% of GDP
Step 1 Gains from removal of barriers affecting trade	8–9	0.2–0.3
Step 2 Gains from removal of barriers affecting overall production	57–71	2.0–2.4
Gains from removing barriers (sub-total)	65–80	2.2–2.7
Step 3 Gains from exploiting economies of scale more fully	61	2.1
Step 4 Gains from intensified competition reducing business inefficiencies and monopoly profits	46	1.6
Gains from market integration (sub-total)	62*–107	2.1*–3.7
Total For 7 member states at 1985 prices	127–187	4.3–6.4
For 12 member states at 1988 prices	174–258	4.3–6.4
Mid-point of above	216	5.3

* This alternative estimate for the sum of steps 3 and 4 cannot be broken down between the two steps.

Source: Commission of EC, study of Directorate-General for Economic and Financial Affairs

Notes: The ranges for certain lines represent the results of using alternative sources of information and methodologies. The seven member states (West Germany, France, Italy, United Kingdom, Benelux) account for 88 per cent of the GDP of the EC twelve. Extrapolation of the results in terms of the same share of GDP for the seven and twelve member states is not likely to over-estimate the total for the twelve. The detailed figures in the table relate only to the seven member states because the underlying studies mainly covered those countries.

But it is the services area – insurance, banking and air and road transport – that Cecchini believes is particularly ill-served by specific market regulations which impede competition. The report points to widely different charges for banking, insurance and brokerage services (see pp. 16–17). Integrating these services, the report says, could save the consumer more than 22 billion ecu (£15.4 billion) in annual charges. This is based on calculations which show that potential and expected price falls for financial services could be as high as 26 per cent (for Spain) or anything between 2 and 12 per cent for the UK.

Potential and expected price falls for financial services			
	Potential price falls (%)	Range of expected price falls	Mid points of the expected range of price falls (%)*
1. Spain	34	16–26	21
2. Italy	28	9–19	14
3. France	24	7–17	12
4. Belgium	23	6–16	11
5. West Germany	25	5–15	10
6. Luxembourg	17	3–13	8
7. UK	13	2–12	7
8. Netherlands	9	0– 9	4

Ranges of 10 percentage points wide have been assumed, with the above expected price falls as the mid points.
Source: The Cecchini Report

The Cecchini Report suggests that the largest overall benefits of the single market in financial services will be felt in the UK and West Germany, where price falls, though relatively modest, are expected to be leveraged upwards by the size of their financial markets. The report estimates that the gain in consumer surplus resulting from the integration of European credit and insurance markets could be as high as 5.1 billion ecu (£3.6 billion) in the UK compared with 4.6 billion ecu (£3.2 billion) in West Germany and 3.7 billion ecu (£2.6 billion) in France.

On a more macro level the Cecchini Report estimates that the impact of cheaper credit as a result of market integration and increased competition could contribute an extra 1.5 per cent to the Community GDP. The deflationary impact on price levels is estimated at about 1.4 per cent and, as a result of a reduction in the debt burden, public finances could improve by as much as 1 per cent of GDP. In the medium term, the report suggests that all this will lead to the creation of nearly 500,000 new jobs.

But before the UK's business community starts popping the champagne corks at the prospect of cheaper credit it must be stressed

Percentage differences in prices of standard financial products compared with the average of the four lowest national prices*

Name of standard service	Description of standard service	West Germany	UK	Spain	Netherlands	Luxembourg	Italy	France	Belgium
Banking services									
Consumer credit	Annual cost of consumer loan of 500 ecu. Excess interest rate over money market rates.	136	121	39	31	−26	121	n.a.	−41
Credit cards	Annual cost assuming 500 ecu debit. Excess interest rate over money market rates.	60	16	26	43	−12	89	−30	79
Mortgages	Annual cost of home loan of 25,000 ecu. Excess interest rate over money market rates.	57	−20	118	−6	n.a.	−4	78	31
Letters of credit	Cost of letter of credit of 50,000 ecu for three months.	−10	8	59	17	27	9	−7	22
Foreign exchange drafts	Cost to a large commercial client of purchasing a commercial draft for 30,000 ecu.	31	16	196	−46	33	23	56	6
Travellers cheques	Cost to a private consumer of purchasing 100 ecu of travellers' cheques.	−7	−7	30	33	−7	22	39	35
Commercial loans	Annual cost (including commissions and charges) to a medium sized firm of a commercial loan of 250,000 ecu.	6	46	19	43	6	9	−7	−5

Insurance services								
Life insurance Average annual cost of term (life) insurance.	78	33	83	66	−9	37	−30	5
Home insurance Annual cost of fire and theft cover for house valued at 70,000 ecu with 28,000 ecu contents.	−16	39	81	57	17	−4	90	3
Motor insurance Annual cost of comprehensive insurance, 1.6 litre car, driver 10 years experience, no claims bonus.	30	9	148	77	−7	100	−17	15
Commercial fire and theft Annual cover for premises valued at 387,240 ecu and stock at 232,344 ecu.	−9	153	245	−15	−1	24	27	43
Public liability cover Annual premium for engineering company with 20 employees and annual turnover of 1.29 million ecu.	13	117	77	9	−16	60	−7	47
Brokerage services								
Private equity transactions Commission costs of cash bargain of 1,440 ecu.	36	−13	−3	7	114	65	123	7
Private gilts transactions Commission costs of cash bargain of 14,000 ecu.	14	21	−63	27	161	217	36	90
Institutional equity transactions Commission costs of cash bargain of 288,000 ecu.	26	−5	47	68	26	153	−47	69
Institutional gilt transactions Commission costs of cash bargain of 7.2 million ecu.	284	57	92	−36	21	60	n.a.	−4

* The figures show the extent to which financial product prices, in each country, are above a low reference level. Each of these price differences implies a theoretical potential price fall from existing price levels to the low reference level.

Source: The Cecchini Report

that there are many unknowns. What is not known is just how quickly the increased competition will filter through to reduced charges and commissions. Interest rates are out of everybody's hands and even the Commission has avoided the issue, knowing that these rates are usually bound up in the economic and monetary policies of each member state.

Estimated gain in consumer surplus resulting from integration of European credit and insurance markets	
	billion ecus
Belgium	0.7
France	3.7
Italy	4.0
Luxembourg	0.1
Netherlands	0.3
Spain	3.2
UK	5.1
West Germany	4.6
Total	21.7
Source: The Cecchini Report	

Moreover, despite market integration and despite the comprehensive package of advice and financial services available to customers from their banks, these institutions still need to use correspondents throughout the Community. Even if breaking down cultural and traditional barriers to consumer banking across twelve disparate nations were feasible, the cost of a Community network for any single bank would be prohibitively expensive. And for businesses watching their cash flow, there is little indication that an integrated financial services market will bring down correspondent banking charges (let alone speed up the payment system) in the foreseeable future.

Forms of payment are not expected to change, the most popular continuing to be payment on open account. Documentary credits may disappear with the breaking down of frontier controls.

Payment charges vary widely as the table on p. 19 shows. The figures are based on remittances in the remitting bank's currency and paid in the same currency to an account in the bank's books in the UK. The correspondent charges are based on a sampling of two or more tariffs.

Undoubtedly, one of the most important breakthroughs for the creation of the single market is the eventual freeing of foreign exchange controls across the Community (see Appendix 2). But business will have to continue hedging foreign exchange risks for many years to come, although those risks are unlikely ever to be substantial between currencies within the exchange rate mechanism of the European Monetary System (EMS).

Payments received (inland payments currency)				
Country	Amount (£)	Method	Typical UK bank charge (£)	Correspondent charge (£)
France	500 5,000 12,000	Urgent/standard	3.00	Free
Greece	500 5,000 12,000	Urgent/standard	3.00	Free
Spain	500 5,000 12,000	Urgent/standard	3.00	6.00 min./no max.
West Germany	500 5,000 12,000	Urgent/standard	3.00	10.00 average
Payments abroad (sterling payments out)				
France	500 5,000 12,000	Urgent/24 hrs max.	6.00 min./30.00 max.	12.00 average
Greece	500 5,000 12,000	Urgent/24 hrs max.	6.00 min./30.00 max.	Unavailable
Spain	500 5,000 12,000	Urgent/24 hrs max.	6.00 min./30.00 max.	6.00 min./1 per cent
West Germany	500 5,000 12,000	Urgent/24 hrs max.	6.00 min./30.00 max.	25.00 average

A unified exchange rate or common currency is a long way off, although there is a growing use of the ecu. Certainly there is scope for those in high interest member states borrowing ecu in low interest areas. There will also be increased opportunities to borrow foreign exchange to service assets where the assets are valued in a foreign currency and are being carried on the balance sheet but are being serviced in sterling. The integrated Community banking system will, in time, lead to more businesses opening foreign currency accounts. The exporter and importer can then begin netting receivables and payments within that foreign account.

The year 1992 and beyond will pose a very different operating and business environment from that existing today. Companies need to be aware of all aspects of the change and use the remedies available to them under the directives which are creating the single market. The opportunities are there but so are the dangers for the unwary.

The benefits of monetary union

If you ever decide to embark on a round trip of the EC, you will need to think carefully about currency conversion. According to a recent survey, if you were to begin such a trip with 40,000 Belgian francs, and stop at each border to change your money, you would lose almost half. By the time you had gone full circle and arrived back in Brussels, the BFr 40,000 with which you started would have been eroded by the attentions of money-changers to just BFr 21,300. In fact, it would be worse than that, because the Bureau of European Consumer Organisations which conducted that exercise left Luxembourg out of the calculation because it is locked into the Belgian franc; and it also omitted the Republic of Ireland. But the figures are startling enough, even when incomplete, to make the point that not having a common currency can prove costly to European travellers and, by implication, European businesses.

Along with the absence of a common language, the lack of monetary union is an obvious reason why it has proved so hard to create a genuine single market. One of the greatest competitive advantages enjoyed by the USA is that it has a common currency; consequently, there are voices in Europe repeatedly pressing the case for monetary integration. The first hurdles are to liberalise the movement of capital across borders (which 1988's Capital Movements Directive hopes to achieve) and to get all member states to join the European Monetary System and its exchange rate mechanism. This would be followed by the adoption of the ecu as a true single European currency, and the formation of a European Central Bank.

The advantages of a single monetary system – besides avoiding the losses incurred by foreign exchange charges illustrated above – are that the stabilisation of exchange rates would reduce currency risks associated with trading, and a common monetary policy should help keep inflation down in countries hitherto suffering high rates of inflation.

Disadvantages

But there are possible disadvantages of monetary union too. True integration would mean that governments would have less freedom over their own monetary policies. Such restrictions might well mean less inflation and greater financial stability, but the national sovereignty of the member states would be threatened and government agencies would no doubt look at issues other than the macro-economic one. National governments would not be allowed to devalue unilaterally when their economies got out of line. Losing control over determination of exchange rates would mean some loss of control over interest rates, thereby diminishing a government's control over its domestic economy.

Whatever the disadvantages of monetary union, most politicians who truly believe in a single market believe that monetary integration is necessary too. Significant advances have already been made by some member states.

Liberalisation of capital movements

The complete removal of capital controls within the Community is a fundamental part of the process to achieve a single market by 1992. There have been significant developments in this area already (notably the Capital Movements Directive of 1988), although at the time of writing only the UK, West Germany, the Netherlands and Denmark have abolished controls completely.

Italy

Italy, however, in the autumn of 1988 brought its regulations on domestic holdings of foreign currencies into line with most other member states. For example, Italian residents were allowed to buy foreign debt issues with a minimum maturity of six months instead of two years, and companies trading overseas were allowed to raise from 10 per cent to 20 per cent the foreign currency element of their liquid assets.

France

The French are also easing restrictions, so that, for example, the limit on the amount of foreign capital that French companies can hold abroad is to be removed. By mid-1990, at least eight states should have fully liberalised. Greece, Spain, Portugal and the Republic of Ireland have until 1992, although Greece and Portugal may get a further extension of three years. In a crisis, states will be allowed to reintroduce capital controls, but only temporarily and with the approval of the Commission, subject to override by the Council.

Freedom from capital controls, when combined with liberalised trade, may make it more difficult for central bankers in each member state to control money supply. How would they exercise control if much of the money in their country were not theirs, but that of their trading partners? There might be little point in the Bank of England trying to keep a tight rein on the supply of sterling, if Deutschemarks, French francs and other currencies over which it has no control are freely available as a substitute. So central banks could find it difficult to define, let alone set up and keep to, effective monetary supply targets, and to set interest rates at a level which they felt was right for their domestic economy. The Padoa Schioppa report of 1987 stated that free trade, capital mobility and fixed exchange rates were incompatible with independent monetary policies. However, the core countries of the EMS have appeared willing to sacrifice the fourth element – independent monetary policies – in order to achieve the other three.

Proposed liberalisation of capital controls	
February 1988	First stages agreed and implemented for major member states
June 1988	Agreement on second round of liberalisation; EC committee set up to examine monetary union which reported summer 1989 (the Delors Report)
July 1990	Complete abolition of exchange controls in France and Italy
1992	Removal of exchange controls in Spain and the Republic of Ireland
Unspecified	Exchange controls may be removed in Portugal and Greece

The European Monetary System

The EMS was created in 1979 in an attempt to form a zone of monetary stability in the EC. Earlier attempts during the 1970s – the so-called European currency 'snake in the tunnel' – had not achieved much success. The exchange rate mechanism (ERM) of the EMS has fared much better in stabilising exchange rates. Although all twelve member states belong to the EMS, three, including the UK, stand on the sidelines of the ERM.

The ERM works very simply. Currencies are assigned a central parity relative to the ecu and this creates a grid of cross rates. Fluctuations of up to 4.5 per cent are permitted by each participating currency, 2.25 per cent on either side of the central rates. The lira, however, has a wider band of 12 per cent, 6 per cent either side of the central rates.

Under the ERM, currencies are stabilised by member states intervening in the foreign exchange markets at the extreme ends of the bands to keep the grid intact or by other policy measures such as adjusting interest rates; or they can agree on a currency realignment. There have been eleven realignments since the formation of the EMS.

EMS realignments 1979–87			
Date	% central rate movement against ecu		
24 Sep 1979	DM +2	DKr −3	
30 Nov 1979	DKr −5		
23 Mar 1981	L −6		
5 Oct 1981	DM +5½	Fl +5½	Fr −5
	L −3		
22 Feb 1982	BFr −8½	Luxfr −8½	DKr −3
12 Jun 1982	DM +4¼	Fl +4½	Fr −5¾
		L −2¾	
21 Mar 1983	DM +5½	Fl +3½	BFr +1½
	Luxfr +1½	DKr +2½	Fr −2½
	IR£ −3½	L −2½	
21 Jul 1985	L −6	all other currencies +2	
7 Apr 1986	DM +3	Fl +3	DKr +1
	BFr +1	Luxfr +1	Fr −3
4 Aug 1986	IR£ −8		
12 Jan 1987	DM +3	Fl +3	BFr +2
+ indicates revaluation − indicates devaluation			

Essential to the working of the EMS and the maintenance of currency parities is the placing by member states of 20 per cent of their US dollar and gold reserves with the European Monetary Co-operation Fund in exchange for ecus. Ecus can be used within agreed limits for settling the debts incurred by central banks in the operation of the EMS.

Should the UK join the exchange rate mechanism of the EMS?

Commentators have put forward a variety of reasons why the UK has not joined the ERM, including the difficulties of finding the 'right' time and rate at which to join; the loss of independence in economic policy; and because the Government feels that it would make UK interest rates dependent on the sterling/Deutschemark exchange rate. Lack of control over interest rates would, goes the argument, deny the UK a valuable tool for dealing with the domestic economy. It is not just an economic issue, but a political one as well.

The ERM is widely viewed as successful, but would it be if the UK were a member? In the absence of the UK, the weaker currencies of the smaller nations have gathered around the Deutschemark. This means that they also tend to take their cue on other monetary matters from the Bundesbank, West Germany's central bank. They have echoed its monetary restraint and its caution and as a consequence have succeeded in the goal they originally set themselves – to create a zone of monetary stability in Europe. Had the UK been in the ERM, it might have been different. From time to time the two-way pull between the West German and French economies has threatened to pull the system apart. With the UK tugging in a third direction, particularly when sterling was inflated by the oil price boom at the beginning of the 1980s, the strains might have been too much.

After the 1987 general election, the Chancellor of the Exchequer indicated that joining the ERM was something that could be considered on its merits. The debate has developed within the Cabinet, but for the moment it seems unlikely that the UK will participate.

Generally speaking, the City would prefer the UK to become a member because it believes that it would make it easier to attract business into the EC from non-member countries. This belief has been strengthened since the leading member states broadly agreed to lift restrictions on capital movements as a major step towards the creation of a unified internal financial market.

Corporate treasurers
There can be little doubt that most UK corporate treasurers would welcome the stability in exchange rates the ERM would be expected to bring. It would save on the costs of hedging exposures, assist the accuracy of financial planning and provide greater certainty about the viability of international projects. It can also be argued that if the UK were in the ERM it would help lower UK inflation, which is one of the highest in the EC, and improve the balance of payments deficit. The European League for Economic Co-operation, for example, argued in late 1988 that the UK should join the ERM for the above reasons, as well as to help the cause of monetary integration.

What is the ecu?

The increasing use of the ecu, an embryonic common currency, is a positive sign of the move towards greater monetary union. The ecu is made up of specified amounts of the individual currencies of member states, excluding (until September 1989) Spain's peseta and Portugal's escudo. In each ecu there is (as of mid-1989) 0.72 Deutschemarks, 3.71 French francs and 8.8 sterling pence. Note that sterling, though not in the adjustment mechanism, is used in the ecu.

Structure of the European Currency Unit (ecu) in 1988		
	Composition	Weight*
Deutschemark	0.719	34.5
French franc	3.71	18.6
Pound sterling	0.088	13.6
Dutch guilder	0.256	10.9
Italian lira	140	9.1
Belgian franc	3.71	8.8
Danish krone	0.219	2.7
Greek drachma	1.15	0.7
Irish punt	0.0087	1.1
Luxembourg franc	0.14	—

* The Spanish peseta and Portuguese escudo will be included in the ecu at its next reweighting, scheduled for September 1989.

The composition of the ecu was not arrived at arbitrarily. It reflects, rather, the distribution of trade among EC members, the size of GNP and the importance of trade to each nation. As these change over time, so the component amounts of the ecu are examined, and, if necessary, revised every five years. The next revision is in September 1989, when the Spanish peseta and the Portugese escudo will be incorporated. These factors produce the internal central rates for the ecu. But, in addition, there is a market rate, from which it is possible to calculate the rate of the ecu against the dollar. This can be used as a yardstick to give parity for each currency against the ecu itself. This rate typically fluctuates.

While the ecu is the centrepiece of the ERM, it is also much more than that. Since 1981 it has been the unit of account of the Commission and it is therefore fundamental to the running of the EC. It is the unit in which the EC sets its budgets. It is also a reserve asset used to settle part of the debts incurred by the central banks of member states in the operation of the EMS.

Accounting in ecus can have the advantage for companies of

allowing them to focus more easily on genuine trading performance rather than being mesmerised by currency fluctuations. For the same reasons, it can be advantageous to borrow in ecus – companies know with reasonable certainty their repayment commitments.

Composition of the ecu			
At 14 March 1979		From September 1989	
Currency	% of ecu	Currency	% of ecu
Deutschemark	27.8	Deutschemark	25.8
French franc	22.1	French franc	20.9
sterling	12.9	sterling	15.8
lira	12.0	lira	17.3
Belgian franc	9.4	Belgian franc	3.4
guilder	9.2	guilder	5.1
krone	3.0	krone	2.4
drachma	2.3	drachma	1.2
punt	1.3	punt	0.7
		escudo	0.8
		peseta	6.6

The ecu also meets a genuine need among borrowers and investors and, as a result, it is now the seventh most popular currency in which to denominate Eurobonds. The UK government recently issued Treasury Bills denominated and payable in ecu. Ecu deposits are also growing. Borrowers from the weaker EMS countries get considerably lower interest rates when they borrow in ecu than on their domestic markets, and they also get an added degree of exchange-rate protection. London is the second largest centre for ecu trading business, after Paris.

Despite these advances, the ecu is still a parallel currency. The use of the ecu in the market place is not considered as great a unifying force as increased exchange-rate stability through the ERM has been. Indeed, a parallel currency can be more de-stabilising than helpful, by adding to the number of currencies already in circulation. Moreover, those responsible for the ecu have no power to influence total monetary conditions in the EC. Nevertheless, the ecu has its uses as a parallel currency and, in so far as it has reflected the choices of market participants, it should be welcomed.

Towards a European Central Bank

More politicians are beginning to believe that for there to be a true single market there should be a supranational financial institution – a European Central Bank. The greater integration of the EC economies will make them more interdependent and it will become progressively harder for governments to go their own way on macro-economic issues.

Although a European Central Bank (ECB) is just an idea at the moment, its main aim would be to maintain prices at similar levels throughout the EC. It would issue and manage a common currency. It would also be the main instrument for co-ordinating all official foreign exchange and money market intervention on behalf of member states. An ECB might also have greater authority to speak on behalf of Community interests at international gatherings. But there is much opposition to the idea of an ECB, from politicians and from national central banks. Such an institution would be independent of national governments and the Commission; and national central banks might become, at best, agencies of the ECB, with no independent monetary power. Not surprisingly, central banks are at the moment generally opposed to being subordinated to a European Central Bank. Besides, such a transfer of responsibilities would raise a substantial number of legal and practical issues in many member states.

In managing a European currency, an ECB would need to have adequate resources available. This means that member states would have to pool substantial proportions of gold and foreign exchange reserves with the bank – as they do to a certain extent with the European Monetary Co-operation Fund. A problem could arise where those that made the highest contributions would want greater influence over the ECB than those that contributed smaller amounts. It might also prove difficult for an ECB to take over national central banks' roles in the functioning of domestic money markets and government finance, and their relationships with banks and other financial institutions. In addition, the location of the ECB could be the source of much rivalry between several EC capital cities. A central bank tends to gather around it other financial institutions, and the location of a central bank usually becomes the financial centre of a country. Even if arrangements were made to share the business among different EC cities, eventually it is likely that the city most closely associated with the Central Bank would become the most dominant in the financial sector. An ECB would also affect each member state's freedom to decide its own fiscal policy. The fiscal policy of a central government may be seriously upset if other levels of government pursue different fiscal policies. Once the power to tax is constrained, then the power of governments to direct their own macro-economic policy is reduced. It has to be said, however, that the reality of the modern deregulated world has already put severe tacit constraints on this policy.

At the time of writing, it is the UK government's view that political integration is not on the European agenda and a European Central Bank implies a degree of political union to which the electorate may not be ready to agree. The creation of a European Central Bank, therefore, requires a political will that appears not to be wholly present. Nevertheless, every move towards monetary integration makes it more possible.

3. Delivery systems, payment methods and advanced electronic systems

Beneath the high technology surface, many international methods of transferring money are essentially the same as those used in the domestic market. Those venturing into exporting for the first time might easily gain the impression that the transfer of funds involves sending cash from one country to another. This, of course, is not the case and money is rarely physically moved. International funds transfers are made by debiting or crediting the accounts that banks hold with one another. International payment instructions are usually transmitted through two or more banks.

The method of payment selected by a company – whether cheque, banker's draft or interbank electronic transfer – will depend as much on the type and size of payment as on other factors, including interest rates, the banking systems of the countries involved, the preferences of the parties concerned in the transaction and the regulations of the importing country. There can be a substantial difference in cost and speed between the methods available. 1992 means that if you are a trader in Bradford and want to export something to Düsseldorf it should prove just as easy – or complicated – as sending it to Brighton. So should receiving money for the goods you have supplied. But will it?

Cheques

If you were dealing with a trader in Brighton you would probably be paid by cheque. An assertion that 'the cheque is in the post' must rank next to 'statistics' as one of the things we mistrust most; moreover, payment by cheque is extremely inefficient. The cheque may get lost in the post and, as a result, there will be a time lag between receiving the cheque and actually having the money in your account –

a delay that can take a few days. This may be good news for the business in Brighton that has to pay you, but it is not good news for you.

When it comes to overseas transactions, receiving money by cheque can have even greater complications. The postal delays between Bradford and Düsseldorf are likely to be much greater than those between Bradford and Brighton, and, in addition, the cheque has to be sent for collection.

Let us assume the cheque you receive from the importer in Düsseldorf is in Deutschemarks. You present it to your bank to obtain payment from the German bank and eventually the cheque becomes pounds sterling in your account. But there will be a bank charge to pay, maybe interest, and you might suffer if there has been a fluctuation in the exchange rate while all this is going on. It is possible to obtain an advance against an uncleared cheque by asking your bank if it is prepared to negotiate the cheque. This involves the bank purchasing the cheque with recourse to you. The bank pays you the money and collects from your importer in Düsseldorf, but should the German cheque bounce, or the bank not receive its money, it will then have recourse to you and charge it against your account. In the end you are liable. It is worth bearing in mind that should the German cheque be returned unpaid, and it has been the subject of a foreign exchange deal, then the bank will recover the unpaid currency amount at the rate of exchange prevailing upon notification that the cheque is unpaid, not the date the cheque was converted into sterling and credited to you. Since there may be quite a delay between the two dates, depending on how exchange rates have fluctuated during that period, this could make a big difference.

However, if you were the importer in Bradford, purchasing goods from a firm in Düsseldorf, it may make sense to pay by cheque. It is relatively cheap, and the money stays in your account until your German exporter goes through the procedure just described. But then given all the work and risk involved, the exporter may not much care to receive your sterling cheque and may favour other methods of payment. So even after 1992 it will not be advisable to buy something from a Düsseldorf firm and just put a sterling cheque in the post. The barriers to trading may have come down, but the German exporter will react to the cheque 'being in the post' just as we do – with scepticism.

Bank drafts

You will be able to continue using bank drafts, long accepted as a standard form of business payment, after 1992. A draft, in sterling or some other currency, offers greater security because it is drawn on a bank not a customer's account, but it still cannot escape postal delay. It is always a good idea to send a draft by registered post because, if a draft you have sent is mislaid or stolen and you ask your bank for a replacement, you will have to provide your bank with an indemnity to cover against financial loss. The reason for this is that, should the missing draft turn up later and be presented for payment, the bank may still have to pay up.

Unlike cheque payments, the moment your bank issues a draft, your account will be debited. If you receive a sterling draft from Düsseldorf then you will only have the normal expense associated with clearing a cheque. If your German importer has sent the draft in Deutschemarks, you will be charged a fee by your bank for collecting the proceeds.

Electronic transfers

Banks already prefer their customers to use an electronic system of payment: it is safer, quicker and more efficient. As 1992 approaches, the emphasis on this will increase. For a transaction with a company in Brighton you could, even now, rely on the Clearing House Automated Payments System (CHAPS); there is a minimum value which CHAPS handles – £7,000 at the time of writing – although this may be reduced in the near future. CHAPS forms an essential link in the electronic transfer of money within the UK, once it has arrived in London from abroad via SWIFT (Society for Worldwide Interbank Financial Tele-communications). Such interbank transfers are the most common method of making international payments and remittances and provide by far the quickest and most effective method of moving funds. This is where CHAPS needs to be SWIFT.

All the major banks in the UK and Europe are members of SWIFT, an international electronic network through which banks transfer funds between one another. In many ways SWIFT acts as an electronic cheque or bank draft but eliminates some of the associated problems. In the classic case, if your importer in Düsseldorf wished to pay you, it would send the necessary instructions to its bank using **Standard/urgent** either a standard transfer or an urgent transfer. The main difference **transfer** between the two lies in the degree of priority to be afforded by the processing bank or the chain of different banks it goes through before you get it. Although urgent transfers cost more than standard transfers, it will still often pay to use urgent transfers, particularly when interest rates are high and the interim borrowing cost incurred while waiting for the standard transfer to arrive can far outweigh the cost of an urgent transfer.

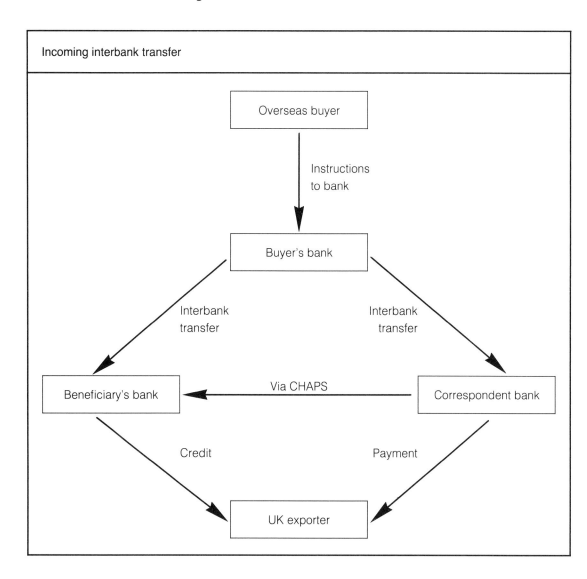

Incoming interbank transfer

An importer in Düsseldorf uses, presumably, a German bank. It is unlikely that the German bank will have an office in Bradford or anywhere else outside London and even the London office is unlikely to have full branch facilities for processing payments. The German bank, however, has an arrangement with a bank in the UK and it is this correspondent bank that receives the electronic transfer from Düsseldorf. The correspondent bank may or may not be the same as your own bank. If it is not, it will use CHAPS to transmit the money to your bank which, in turn, will pass it on to your branch and your account using the bank's internal computer system. When funds are transferred from one country to another in this way, there is no physical movement of money. Cash does not literally move across borders. International transfers of funds are made by debiting and crediting the accounts that the various banks hold with one another.

Value date The money that is received from the correspondent bank will bear what is called a value date. This is the date when funds to cover the payment are made available to the paying bank. The date is of significance because, irrespective of the time the instruction is received, payment cannot be made until the value date. This is because up to that time your importer in Düsseldorf could change his mind and stop the payment.

But while the electronic system has many advantages and it is quicker than anything else, there are many delays that can occur. There could be delays due to local banking conditions or the need to satisfy exchange control regulations. Then there are bank holidays, widely different hours of business and time differences. Banks in the UK and Japan, for example, are never open at the same time, so it is impossible to make a same-day transfer between London and Tokyo. Bank holidays do not coincide in different countries and there are also local holidays to contend with. No matter how sophisticated the electronic system is, there are many practical reasons why delays might occur for even the most urgent payment.

If you want to make or receive payments in ecu, the payments must be in the hands of the paying bank by 11 a.m. local time on the day before the value date quoted. Payment cannot be made, however, if one of the member states whose currency participates in the ecu has a bank holiday on the value date.

Cut-off time After a certain time of day, a time that will vary for payments to different countries and time-zones, banks will be unable to execute payment orders on the day they are received. This is known as cut-off time and your bank should be able to inform you of these.

SWIFT is very cheap. There is currently a very small basic payment per message, irrespective of size or destination and this enables banks to minimise their all-in charge to the customer. The charge can vary from £6 to £30, depending on the message and its urgency, but the service provided for this is fast, secure and efficient.

Certain principles of international trade should always be followed whether you are sending money through the electronic envelope or just through ordinary mail: make sure you have provided your bank with all the details it needs about who is to be paid. If you are expecting money from your customers, then make sure they know all your details. You should provide your full name and address, your bank's name and full address and your account number. It will help if these are printed on the invoice; this has been common practice in some member states – such as West Germany – for many years.

Banking experts are convinced that there is now no going back on SWIFT and electronic banking. 'We could not go back to pre-SWIFT days. The system would collapse if SWIFT stopped,' says one banker. Thankfully, SWIFT does not stop and in any twenty-four-hour period it is available for 99.73 per cent of the time and it averages about a million messages a day.

Electronic Data Interchange

Marvellous as SWIFT is, it is only the tip of that vast iceberg known as Electronic Data Interchange (EDI). Its supporters say that one day it will have the same impact on business as the telephone has had. To quote a well-known phrase, 'You ain't seen nothin' yet'. One expert in this field believes that once EDI gets going it will transform business **Paperless trading** and usher in 'paperless trading'.

The SWIFT system is one of the world's largest EDI networks, though it is available only to banks. But EDI systems go far beyond banks in their application. What stops the business in Bradford and the importer in Düsseldorf from having the whole transaction carried out on computers? Nothing. It is very likely that they already rely on computers a great deal. What probably happens is that an order originates on the Düsseldorf firm's computers which then produce a hard copy and send it by post, telex, fax or some other means to Bradford. This is a bit like writing a letter then reading it out over the telephone. No one would dream of doing that, though it is what most firms do with computers – some 70 per cent of all paper output from one computer is re-keyed into another computer. Not only is such a process wasteful, but it provides scope for mistakes. Sainsbury might deal with 40,000 invoices a week: 25 per cent are wrong and need to be amended or rejected. Letters of credit and other documents submitted to a bank are rarely done properly: between 50 per cent and 80 per cent of such documents are rejected and have to be redone, recalculated, resubmitted.

Standards What is needed is for the computers of the firm in Bradford and the firm in Düsseldorf to talk to each other. For this two things are necessary: the first is a common language – something like a business esperanto. This allows any computer to understand messages before translating them into its own in-house computer dialect. This avoids the need to rewrite all internal programs. If separate dialects were used, there would soon develop an unacceptable translation problem for a supplier who deals with, say, fifty manufacturers. These common dialects are known as standards and they are vital to EDI. The standard will give rules for the construction of messages to match parts of the business process such as order, invoice, payment. These can then be approved and published for use by everyone.

But to implement EDI a communication network is needed in which agreed messages can be passed over the network, with software at each end which can accept and create these messages and link them to the company's internal systems. The communications networks usually operate a mailbox system so that messages are deposited in a mailbox to be collected when convenient. The sending and collection of messages by any one party usually takes place at the same time. This avoids having to be constantly connected to the network, which is expensive. The network can be seen as equivalent to a telephone network and there are three major international networks in operation: the IBM network, ISTEL network and INS-GE Information Services.

So to go back to our example, Bradford might begin with a warning to its sales staff that an order from Düsseldorf is expected. It knows this because Düsseldorf has interrogated Bradford's product catalogue database. This is the electronic equivalent of Düsseldorf asking for a printed catalogue of Bradford's goods, or talking to Bradford's salesmen, or telephoning them with their needs. Bradford may already have background and credit references on Düsseldorf and an initial trading limit may also be assigned. If it has been done in the past, it may be updated on the basis of current trading conditions and experience. Then an electronic transaction file would be opened through which the subsequent quotation, order, delivery and payment messages would be handled automatically.

EDI could also be used by Bradford to organise additional activities such as booking the shipping space, updating currency exposure positions, producing export document sets and instituting packing, delivery and even manufacturing processes. Of course, while all this is going on, internal information systems would be constantly updated. Thus the treasury department of the Bradford firm would be able to obtain an updated position at any time about available funds, funds due or in transmission, or any other aspect of its activities.

Quite clearly similar processes can be set up for transactions between Bradford and Brighton, or if the Bradford firm was providing a service to the Düsseldorf firm, rather than supplying goods. Experts have no doubts that such developments are feasible right across the commercial spectrum. The time between the receipt of the order and the final settlement can take as little as forty-eight hours.

Banks can play a big part in this, because, apart from helping in the settlement process, they can provide a wide range of information, such as credit reference and company data, currency and interest rates and background economic and export data. They can be involved in the insurance arrangements, in collating and processing the export 'documentation', in guaranteeing performance and settlement, as well as supporting any dealing or hedging activity which results from the transaction.

Users
EDI started with the car manufacturers, where its use in maintaining stocks and ordering various parts was quickly appreciated. This led car manufacturers to join together to experiment with EDI and their success led other industries to follow their example. Other industries using EDI now include ports, shipping, electrical components, health services and retail. It is growing in importance in the UK and in Europe. Although there are only about 1,500 users in this country, numbers are growing by between 50 per cent and 150 per cent each year. And the UK is clearly leading the field.

A UK bank recently featured in a unique experiment that linked up Rothmans with P&O. This involved the bank receiving an EDI message that Rothmans was the beneficiary of a documentary credit. Rothmans was informed and it communicated with P&O to arrange shipment of goods. P&O, in turn, sent the bank an EDI message which was effectively a waybill to complete the transactions. Had paper been used, the transaction would have taken four days; using EDI it took only forty-eight hours. The experiment showed the potential of such direct links – a potential that has been appreciated by sixty or seventy of *The Times* Top 100 companies (including ICI, Guinness, British Coal and Trafalgar House), which already use EDI for exchanging information on orders and invoicing and sometimes even for moving goods.

Such uses of EDI are not, of course, directly related to 1992. But the fact that 1992 will mean major changes in the EC will hasten its introduction and make it more meaningful and relevant to business enterprises other than the big companies. 1992 could well provide the spur that EDI needs to be universally accepted and appreciated. The whole issue of information technology and 1992 will be dealt with in a later volume in this series.

4. Short-term trade-related bank facilities

Overdrafts and traditional working finance

Both importers and exporters will find that banks can help them enormously. Although banks provide all sorts of extra services, their main role is simple: to bridge the gap between the date that the exporter wants to be paid and the date the importer wants to pay. The financial terms you agree with your EC buyer are entirely up to you but will reflect your assessment of the trade risk you run in dealing with them.

Fortunately, banks like lending for trade-related transactions because they are usually secure: it is less likely that the bank's money will vanish without trace if it is tied to a particular transaction. So banks are generally happy to provide trade finance and they work hard to improve techniques. Although the basis of trade financing has remained largely unchanged for years, procedures have been streamlined both by the banks and by bodies like the Simplification of International Trade Procedures Board (SITPRO). Add to that the spread of computers, and it is easy to see why the process of financing exports is much easier than it used to be.

How you finance a deal is intimately linked to the method by which you are being paid. There are two key questions to be answered:

- How certain are you that your buyer will pay?

- Will your buyer need to be given a credit?

Choosing the payment method

The financing tool is linked to the payment method, and this in turn depends on the relationship you have with your buyer. Eighty per cent **Open account** of all trade in the EC is carried out on open account; the exporter ships the buyer's goods with an invoice and waits for payment. In the future, especially as the trade barriers come down, it is expected that

Overdraft

even more trade will be on open account. The normal method for covering the manufacturing and shipment period is through an overdraft, which can be in sterling or currency, and opened in the UK or abroad. Factoring or invoice discounting can also be used to provide finance.

Documentary collection/credit

The trouble with open account is that on its own it gives no security to you as seller. You can cover yourself with ECGD (Export Credits Guarantee Department) or a private credit insurance policy but not for the full amount, and you leave yourself open to further delays if you do have to claim. For that reason, open account is advisable only when you have a steady trading relationship with a buyer. For first-time customers the documentary collection route is more sensible. And if there is any possibility of non-payment for political or currency exchange reasons, you should use a documentary credit. Both of these mechanisms can be used to raise money to finance the underlying trade. Nevertheless, the use of documentary collections and documentary credits is on the decline in the Community: partly because of the lower trade risk that comes with greater economic and political stability; partly because goods are often transported faster than the paperwork can be processed; and partly because most trade in the EC is conducted without bills of lading (receipts given by the shipping company or its agent when it accepts the goods), which are documents of title important to the smooth operation of documentary collections and documentary credits.

Giving your customer credit

If your customer badly needs your product, and cannot get it as cheaply from anyone else, then it may have to raise its own finance, usually through loans or overdrafts.

Normally suppliers will give their customers credit. How much you give depends largely on your bargaining position. It may well be that a rival supplier is offering three or six months' free credit: this can be a marketing tool as powerful as a big price-cut. You may have to match this, if necessary building the financing costs into your price.

Buyer credit

For large contracts, particularly projects, overseas buyers may look for a longer credit period, perhaps up to five years. In this case buyer credit can be arranged through a bank and guaranteed by the ECGD. Loans such as these are provided direct to the overseas buyer for up to 85 per cent of the UK content, with the buyer financing the rest of the cost out of its own resources.

Collections and documentary advances

The bank collection system will give you rather more security than open account, while remaining simple and relatively cheap. By offering a term bill of exchange – that is, payable some time in the future – you can also give your buyer credit and, by selling the bill, receive funds immediately. The system is operated by the banks and is controlled by well-established rules.

Term bill of exchange

The main players in the collection process are the exporter, its bank (the remitting bank), the bank's correspondent in the buyer's country (the collecting bank) and the buyer. Documents are passed from one player to the next, after which the importer pays up, or undertakes to pay at an agreed date in the future. The key document is normally the bill of exchange. This is a written demand, signed by the seller, that the buyer (or its bank) should pay a certain amount, either 'at sight', that is immediately, or a number of days (usually between 30 and 180) after sight. This second is called a 'term' or 'usance' bill, and is a way in which the seller can give credit to the buyer. The seller may, however, be able to discount the bill with a bank and obtain immediate cash.

Clean/documentary collection

There are two sorts of collection: clean and documentary. In a clean collection, the only document passed through is the demand for payment, usually a bill of exchange. In a documentary collection, commercial or transport documents – including the bill of lading, which proves the goods have been shipped – are attached to the bill of exchange. The holder of the bill of lading controls title to the goods, but the banks hold it during the collection process, and this gives more security to the exporter.

In contrast to the even safer documentary credit route (see pp. 40–44), the banks can make only a cursory check of the documents as they will have no knowledge of the requirements of the contract between the trading parties and will not be incurring a financial risk.

The procedure is simple. After the exporter has shipped goods, the documents are sent to the remitting bank. These are then sent on to the collecting bank, which will either ask the importing company to come and inspect the documents, or will simply send them to it 'in trust'. The buyer should pay immediately, if the bill is payable at sight, or will 'accept' the bill by signing it. The bank keeps it until it is due for payment, then presents it for payment. The proceeds are then sent to the exporter, usually via the remitting bank.

Problems

There are problem areas that should be noted. First, the collecting bank may be slow in pressing the buyer for payment – especially if it is a customer. Second, on short voyages, the documents may arrive after the goods, in which case they may have to be warehoused. This problem is exacerbated if the seller does not send all the documents off immediately after shipment. Major UK banks have been working on this question, and have developed schemes – often using micro-computers – that enable documents to be sent through much faster. Computers can also be used to monitor whether and when payments have been made.

Finance

Documentary advance

There are two main ways of financing collection transactions. If the importer is required to pay at sight, that is, as soon as the documents arrive, the exporter can ask its bank for a documentary advance. This is a loan based on a percentage of the value of collections outstanding and is appropriate for exporters using collections regularly. When the business is insured through ECGD, the bank may want to have the policy's benefits assigned to it. It is, of course, important to discuss financing needs with the bank well in advance.

Where payment is at sight, or on a term basis, the exporter can ask its bank to negotiate, or purchase, the bill of exchange at the time it is sent for collection. The amount received depends on the length of time before payment. If the buyer does not pay, however, any loss will have to be borne by the exporter unless insured against such risk.

Documentary credits and bill discounts

Letter of credit

Where you do not have an established trading relationship with a customer, it is safest to ask them to open a documentary credit, commonly called a letter of credit or l/c. Most exporters to developing countries rely on documentary credits, and even within the EC it is safer to use them in the early stages of a trading relationship. After a while, you should be able to move on to a collection or open account basis, as documentary credits provide rather more work for the importer, and some extra expense for yourself. If you are competing for business, and other factors are equal, it is likely that an importer will prefer the supplier who is not requesting an l/c. In this case, it is worth taking the advice of your bank before making a decision.

Because the l/c is a secure form of payment if it has been under-written (or confirmed) by a UK bank, it is possible to draw a term bill on that bank, under an acceptance credit. This can be discounted at a prime market rate, and provides a relatively low-cost source of finance for the exporter.

A documentary l/c gives security to both sides. It is, however, a cumbersome mechanism to use within the EC and is relatively uncommon. As trade barriers are lifted it will probably become more so. By interposing a bank as an intermediary, the importer is not required to pay for the goods until documents specified in the l/c have been presented, while the exporter has the comfort that payment is assured if the documents are presented correctly. The documents and terms of the l/c will reflect the agreed trading terms between the importer and exporter.

What is a documentary credit?

The definition of an l/c is simple. It is a written undertaking given by a bank on behalf of the importer to pay the exporter an amount of money within a specified time, provided the seller presents documents strictly in accordance with the l/c. As soon as the importer's bank receives documentation proving that goods have been shipped according to the contract, it will pay the exporter, normally through a bank in the exporter's country. Since the issue of the l/c can obligate the importer's bank to make a payment at some future time, the bank will include the financial liability in its risk assessment of the importer; the bank's willingness to issue an l/c cannot therefore be assumed and issue may restrict the importer's ability to raise other lines of finance.

L/c variations   There are several variations on l/cs. The first choice is whether an l/c is revocable or irrevocable. As a revocable l/c can be cancelled or amended by the issuing bank, it gives little security to the exporter and is rarely used. The second choice is whether it is confirmed or not. Although an l/c may allow the bank in the importer's country to make payment, there may be problems that stop the money getting through. In this case, the exporter can ask for the credit to be confirmed by a bank in his own country, so that it will pay up regardless of whether the money has been received from the issuing bank. This is a form of insurance, and so costs money. However, where the exporter considers the risk high, the use of an irrevocable confirmed letter of credit is a sensible option.

As banks rely on the documentation, and do not involve themselves in the actual goods or underlying contract, they must be certain that the documentation is correct, and may refuse to pay simply because there is a spelling mistake in the paperwork. It is up to the exporter to ensure that there are no mistakes, and this has been made easier by the steady simplification of documents pushed through by bodies like the

Simplification of International Trade Procedures Board (SITPRO). Increasingly, computers are being used to prepare paperwork, and the most sophisticated l/c users – for example, companies importing quantities of clothing from the Far East – can handle most of the documentation without touching 'hard copy'.

To ensure that standard l/c procedures are followed throughout the world, the International Chamber of Commerce has produced detailed guidelines called *Uniform Customs and Practice for Documentary Credits*. This is the key text for all involved in l/cs – only a handful of countries are not signatories to it – and copies are held at most bank branches.

How do documentary credits work?

The most complicted sort of l/c is a confirmed irrevocable letter of credit.

Example

The Mowemdown Lawnmower Company of Birmingham wins an order to supply 200 machines to Belborg AG of Belborg, West Germany. Mowemdown has not supplied Belborg before because Belborg is a new company without an established trading record. For this reason, Mowemdown requires Belborg to have its bank issue an irrevocable confirmed documentary credit.

Mowemdown and Belborg draw up a contract of sale: its main points cover the price (and whether that includes insurance and freight costs), shipping period, what the goods are, method of payment (i.e. a documentary credit payable in sterling at sight and confirmed in London), how the goods are to be shipped, the documents required and the name of the seller's bank.

Belborg then applies to its bank (the issuing bank) to issue a documentary credit. This will include certain details of the contract of sale, and an instruction to the bank to telex or mail full details to the seller through the exporter's bank (the advising bank), asking it to add its confirmation to the credit. If the issuing bank is willing to undertake the obligation on Belborg's behalf and is satisfied with the details of the credit, it passes them on to the advising bank, which in turn advises the credit (with its confirmation) to Mowemdown. Mowemdown should study this carefully, to check that it reflects the contents of the contract of sale. It must also make sure that it can comply with the credit requirements.

If Mowemdown decides that (to look at the sample opposite), it cannot get the lawnmowers to Germany in one go, it immediately asks Belborg AG to delete the 'partshipment prohibited' clause. This amendment will only become effective when it has been passed to Mowemdown by the advising bank.

Having shipped its lawnmowers, Mowemdown presents the documents specified to the advising bank. It sends a covering letter, which lists the documents enclosed, the documentary credit reference, and says how it wants to be paid. If the advising bank is happy with the documents – in this case, a sight draft (a demand for payment under the terms of the credit, signed by the seller), invoices, insurance certificate and a complete set of bills of lading – it will pay up immediately.

Specimen documentary credit

National Westminster Bank PLC ♻

International Trade Services
Documentary Credits Department
National Westminster Tower
25 Old Broad Street
London EC2N 1HQ

Direct Line 01-920
Switchboard 01-920 5555   Telex 885361 NWBLDN G

Mowemdown Lawnmower Co Ltd
Razor Edge Road
Birmingham

Dear Sirs

We have been requested by Traders Bank of Belborg, Belborg, Germany to advise
the issue of their irrevocable Credit Number 01/765 in your favour for account
of Belborg AG c/o EC Line, 1 Euro Strasse, Belborg, Germany for £100,000 (SAY
ONE HUNDRED THOUSAND POUNDS STERLING).

Available by your drafts on us at .... sight accompanied by the
following documents namely:

1. Signed Invoices in triplicate certifying goods are in accordance with
    Contract No. 1234 dated 24 October 1988 between Belborg AG and Mowemdown
    Lawnmower Co Ltd.

2. Marine and War Risk Insurance Certificate covering "all risks" warehouse
    to warehouse, for 10% above the CIF value, evidencing that claims are
    payable in Germany.

3. Complete set 3/3 Shipping Company's clean "on board" ocean Bills of Lading
    made out to order of the shippers and endorsed to order of "Traders Bank
    of Belborg", marked "Freight Paid" and "Notify Belborg AG c/o EC Line,
    1 Euro Strasse, Belborg, Germany".

Covering: Lawnmowers CIF Belborg, Germany.

Shipped from UK Port to Belborg, Germany.

Partshipment prohibited   Transhipment prohibited

Documents must be presented for payment within 15 days from the date of shipment.

We are requested to add our confirmation to this Credit and we hereby undertake to pay you the face amount of your drafts drawn within its terms provided
such drafts bear the number and date of the Credit and that the Letter of
Credit and all amendments thereto are attached.

The Credit is subject to Uniform Customs and Practice for Documentary Credits
(1983 Revision), International Chamber of Commerce Publication No. 400

Drafts drawn under this   [X] Payment   ⎫
Credit must be presented to us for   [ ] Negotiation ⎬not later than 14 December 1988
                                     [ ] Acceptance ⎭

and marked "Drawn under Credit Number 01/765/NWB/2A of Traders Bank of Belborg
Belborg, Germany   Dated 1 November 1988

Discounting

Acceptance credit

Had Mowemdown agreed to give Belborg AG credit, the sight draft would have been replaced by a draft drawn on the advising/confirming bank, demanding payment at a future date ('at ninety days sight', for example). Instead of paying immediately, the bank returns the draft annotated with its acceptance by which it undertakes to pay ninety days hence. This credit is called an acceptance (or sometimes a term or usance) credit.

Deferred payment credit

Mowemdown could discount the draft, meaning it would get paid immediately, with ninety days' interest at the finest rate deducted. Most banks will discount their own acceptances at up to 180 days, and sometimes longer. In the EC, it is common practice for documentary credits to be issued deferring payment, but without calling for the seller to draw a draft: this is known as a deferred payment credit. The advising bank will provide a letter to the exporter saying that the issuing bank agrees to pay in ninety days.

This does not of itself provide a discount facility. However, if the credit is confirmed, a letter from the advising bank undertaking to pay on the due date may be sufficient to enable the exporter to obtain an advance.

Credit insurance

Credit insurance is more than simply a way of protecting receivables. It can play a crucial role in providing finance for growth. If you show your bank manager that you have credit protection and that any new business your sales force can generate will also be covered, you stand a much better chance of getting the finance you need. From your bank's point of view, you will be a better risk. Insurance may enable you to raise money at finer rates from your bank, although you must remember that the premium is part of the overall financing cost.

Traditionally, the underwriting of credit insurance in the UK has fallen into two distinct areas: domestic and foreign. The domestic business has been dominated by private companies, chiefly Trade Indemnity (although TI insures export credits too). The foreign (including EC) business goes largely to the Government's Export Credits Guarantee Department (ECGD), which does not offer domestic credit insurance. Alongside TI are other private underwriters offering both domestic and foreign credit insurance. They include American International Group (AIG) and PanFinancial, which offers

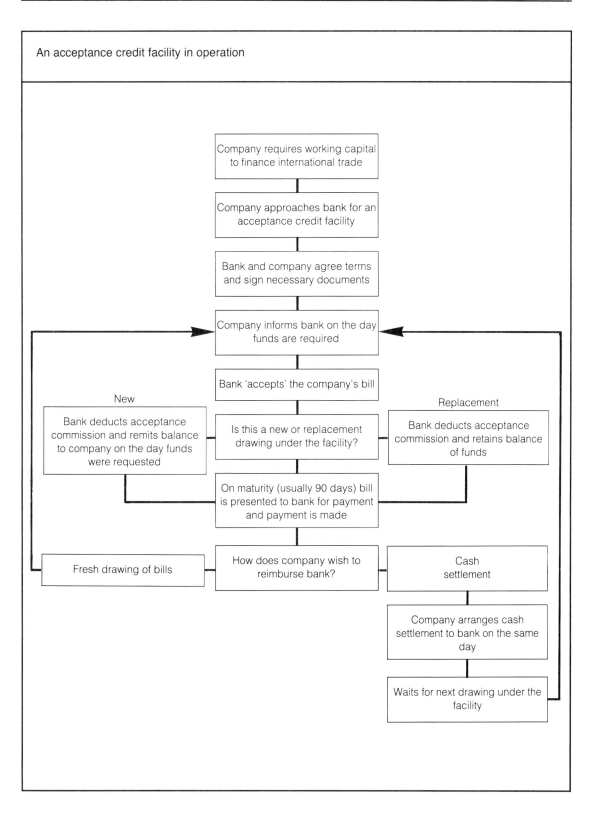

An acceptance credit facility in operation

Company requires working capital to finance international trade

Company approaches bank for an acceptance credit facility

Bank and company agree terms and sign necessary documents

Company informs bank on the day funds are required

Bank 'accepts' the company's bill

New — Bank deducts acceptance commission and remits balance to company on the day funds were requested

Is this a new or replacement drawing under the facility?

Replacement — Bank deducts acceptance commission and retains balance of funds

On maturity (usually 90 days) bill is presented to bank for payment and payment is made

Fresh drawing of bills

How does company wish to reimburse bank?

Cash settlement

Company arranges cash settlement to bank on the same day

Waits for next drawing under the facility

specialist insolvency catastrophe insurance to protect against the default of a major customer.

Risk in the Community

A recent ECGD publication noted that 'being part of the single European market will not remove the risk of buyer default or insolvency from export transactions' and that as a result 'ECGD services will be more necessary than ever'. There are 80,000 bankruptcies a year in the EC, creating a mountain of debt against which a modest premium for an ECGD policy would provide protection. Of the £11 billion of UK exports covered by ECGD last year, 43 per cent was for exports to other member states.

Credit insurers in future

The Commission is working on proposals to adapt the export credit insurance market to the changes that will come about after 1 July 1990. Several major questions will have to be resolved. For instance, should the EC have a pan-European export credit agency to provide credit insurance and support for bank finance schemes in all member states? If such an agency were created, should it be allowed to borrow funds in its own right so that it can act as an export bank, lending money direct to exporters; or should it follow the ECGD model of issuing guarantees to banks to enable them to provide the finance? Will the state-run credit insurers be able to restrict cover to companies in their own country, or will they have to offer cover to companies from throughout the EC? Will the private sector insurers, which may have to meet certain EC requirements on reserves, be at an unfair disadvantage to the state agencies, which with their larger capital resources will not be under the same constraints?

A previous proposal to create a European export credit agency was opposed by member states because they said it would undermine their sovereignty and not provide any new finance. The climate is now more favourable, one attraction being that a harmonised and co-ordinated system would help European companies to band together to win large contracts in non-member states.

The imminent arrival of 1992 has shaken up both ECGD and TI. In the short term, it has led to strong competition for foreign business, and so to lower premiums. The status and operations of ECGD in the single market have been the subject of an inquiry to discuss whether it should remain a government department or become a semi-privatised agency. Whatever future form ECGD takes, and despite the fact that the Commission will want to regard the EC as a single 'domestic' market after 1992, ECGD will continue to provide credit insurance for UK exports to other member states.

Brokers

While you can deal directly with these underwriters, it often makes sense to talk first to a broker, who will advise you which company will suit you best. If your general broker does not handle credit insurance, speak to your bankers, who should be able to recommend a specialist firm. In any event, you should tell your bank who your insurance broker is so that they can work together if you do make a claim.

Which underwriter?

The leading insurer for UK exporters is ECGD. The short-term department, called the Insurance Services Group, is based in Cardiff. It has been making huge investments in information technology and can now give a response to more than 70 per cent of queries on EC business on the same day. The main advantage of using ECGD is that bankers are familiar with its documentation and it offers the security of dealing with an organisation whose ultimate backer is the Government; the spread of its regional offices can also be helpful.

ECGD's main competitor is TI; the size of its export business is small, relative to ECGD, but growing. If you already use domestic credit insurance, it might be worth asking for details of TI's export schemes.

How does credit insurance work?

Example

Colourshoot makes up slide transparencies into educational filmstrips. It has a turnover of around £1 million. Most of its business goes to government departments or advertising agencies in Britain. With customers like these, Colourshoot does not bother with credit insurance. The company has a good credit control department for its few smaller customers and the security of payment of the major part of the business keeps the bank happy.

Suddenly, Colourshoot gets an inquiry from an Italian company for an order that could double turnover. But to fulfil the order Colourshoot will have to increase its capacity immediately – a capital investment of some £50,000 – and increase its staff.

The customer appears to be creditworthy but Colourshoot's bank is wary, and is unwilling to lend for expansion unless the firm takes out credit insurance. The bank's trade finance unit is able to introduce a broker: before selecting any particular cover, Colourshoot is advised to review its plans for doing business in the EC. If business is likely to increase, the identity of the new customers may make a difference to the sort of policy that should be chosen.

Both ECGD and the private underwriters provide individual contract or whole turnover cover, or something in between. If Colourshoot decides it is likely to expand its export business, individual contract cover may not be the most suitable now. That is just the first choice; ECGD, in particular, has a vast range of schemes. Cover can, for example, be arranged from the date of contract or from the date of despatch. It can also cover contracts denominated in foreign currencies. The policy will normally cover 90 per cent of commercial risk – that is, non-payment by the buyer – and 95 per cent of political risk. If, for example, a run on an EC currency were to cause that government to impose exchange controls (a situation which is, admittedly, less likely to occur as trade barriers are lifted), the buyer may be willing to pay in local currency but be unable to remit it abroad; in this case, Colourshoot would still get 95 per cent of its money from ECGD.

Although a company such as Colourshoot will probably want only the simplest of cover at this stage – that is, just for the individual contract – Eurocolour, its larger competitor, will take advantage of other policies. It already has a small subsidiary in Paris and associated companies in Italy and West Germany, together with a warehousing arrangement in Madrid. ECGD covers contracts with all these.

As 1992 approaches, Eurocolour is also expanding its proportion of goods made in the EC outside the UK. ECGD can cover sales of these foreign goods made by the UK company in other member states.

Short-term export finance schemes

The cover provided by the range of insurance policies issued by export credit agencies makes obtaining export finance easier, but difficulties can still arise in the short term. The banks have recognised this problem and now offer a range of short-term finance schemes giving exporters finance for credit periods up to two years. Furthermore, many of the schemes incorporate a limitation on the extent of recourse to the exporter in the event of non payment and, in some cases, finance can be provided totally free of recourse.

Following the withdrawal of the Comprehensive Banker's Guarantee Scheme by ECGD in 1987, many banks developed their own range of services. The schemes available vary considerably from bank to bank but are similar in so far as the banks supply funds on evidence of shipment or other documentation, such as an invoice.

The precise terms offered will depend on the size of a company's export turnover, the markets involved, the methods of settlement normally used and typical invoice amounts. The schemes have been designed to meet and ease the exporter's worries about payments for his goods, to reduce paperwork and generally facilitate the exporter's way in the market place.

The schemes the banks offer are aimed at all levels of exporter. For smaller companies who do not have an export credit insurance policy, the banks can insure shipments under their own policies. As shipments are made the exporter receives payment from his bank, he then assigns to the bank the payments due from the buyer. Both the exporter and the bank can select the business to be financed. The credit period would normally be for a maximum of 180 days with an advance of up to 90 per cent or possibly 100 per cent of the transaction value, depending on which bank's scheme is used. Such schemes can be utilised for a wide range of payment terms. The small exporter benefits from immediate payment on shipment and simplicity of administration.

To assist medium-sized businesses who are willing to offer all (or an approved selection) of their contracts for finance and insurance, several options exist. Exporters may either manage their own insurance policy or they may be invited to become a joint insured party in their own bank's policy. Such schemes are available to companies whatever their terms of trading but subject to the conditions of their export credit insurance cover. The benefits of utilising a bank's policy will include a credit period of up to 180 days although, exceptionally, for appropriate goods, up to two years may be granted. Foreign currency finance is available and the banks handle all the necessary paperwork. Once the buyer accepts the bill, note, or goods if on open account, then there is no recourse to the exporter providing he fulfils his own contractual obligations.

Where companies hold their own credit insurance policy, they may be joined in this policy by their financier. The financier having the comfort of this insurance policy is able to provide finance for insured transactions; which can be provided in a wide range of currencies at fixed or floating rates of interest. There may also be other methods of finance available from some banks.

Export invoice discounting

Export invoice discounting schemes offer an attractive method of obtaining finance on short-term export debts, i.e. open account debts which should be paid in 90 days or less. Schemes such as these are particularly suitable for exporters selling to the EC, North America and other markets which are suitable for open account trading and which involve a low political risk. The invoice discounting arrangements have the advantage that the sale of the book debts is not disclosed to the overseas buyers. Invoice discounting involves the sale of the trade debtor asset by the exporter to the invoice discounting company. It is not a borrowing arrangement and therefore does not involve a charge over the book debts. Payment of up to 80 per cent of the value of invoices is made available to the exporter immediately, with the balance of 20 per cent (less the discounting company's charges) being received when the overseas customer pays. Discounting companies normally require sales of at least £1 million per annum to be discounted. Most agreements are with recourse to the exporter, although some discounters offer bad debt protection. Invoices in foreign currency are acceptable, but political risks are not normally covered.

In order to help medium-sized to large companies gain access to difficult markets they may in certain cases obtain confirming finance and seek cover under the ECGD confirming house policy held by their bank. There is usually a minimum buyer facility sterling amount (or foreign currency equivalent). The maximum credit period is usually 180 days (up to two years may be granted for appropriate goods in exceptional circumstances). Finance is normally available for 100 per cent of the transaction in a wide range of currencies at fixed or floating interest rates.

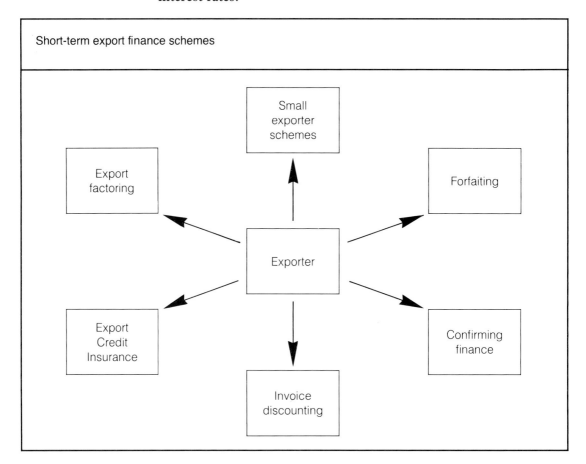

Short-term export finance schemes

Export credit insurance can be provided by ECGD and a wide range of private sector companies, including Trade Indemnity. In addition, political risk insurance can be obtained through the Lloyd's Insurance Market. The acceptability of such cover to banks may vary and therefore each should be approached individually for details of the cover they accept.

Other schemes

Performance bond

Some foreign buyers may also require you to post a bond. This is relatively rare in the EC, although government agencies may sometimes require one. For example, the Italian buyer in the Colourshoot example may know that Colourshoot will have to invest to fulfil the contract. So it may require a bond from your bank, issued on your behalf, as security that the order will be delivered on time. A performance bond of this sort can be an expensive strain on your credit lines as the bank will probably view its risk on the bond and your overdraft in much the same light. Fortunately, ECGD can cover this risk if it is also insuring the underlying contract.

Factoring

Factoring provides a source of working capital which can be used by a company instead of an overdraft or a loan to bridge the gap between invoicing and receiving payment. It is used for both domestic and international trade. A factoring house (which is usually owned by a bank) will buy a company's trade debts and make finance available immediately, thus providing the company with working capital. The factor also provides useful services such as credit checking all the company's new and existing customers, taking over the running of the company's sales ledger and taking responsibility for collecting the debt from the company's customers. Some factors provide bad debt protection on approved debts, others do not. Factoring is therefore a form of instant finance and bad debt protection, which saves the supplier the trouble of pursuing his buyers for payment.

These benefits are particularly attractive to small and growing companies which frequently find themselves suffering from cash-flow problems (see the B&W case study, pp. 124–5). A common feature of rapid growth is that as sales increase, the cash necessary to finance those sales can dry up, and over-trading can result.

Overdrafts are almost always the business's first method of raising finance but they are, technically, repayable on demand. In addition, security is often required, sometimes involving the business owner putting the family home on the line. Factoring is a useful alternative because the finance it provides, being geared to sales, automatically matches the rate at which the company grows. As the sales increase in value, so does the amount pre-paid by the factor.

How does factoring work?

The factoring company pre-pays the company an agreed percentage of the value of sales. This percentage can be up to 80 per cent. When the trade customer pays the full amount to the factor at the end of the normal credit period, the balance of sales still owed to the company is paid by the factor. The factoring charges to the company consist of interest on the finance used at more or less the normal bank overdraft rate (sometimes up to 0.5 per cent more), plus a charge for the accounting services, collection services and bad debt protection. An advantage of these additional services is that they release staff from chasing up customer accounts and free management to promote and run the business.

Generally speaking, factoring companies will only take on firms that have an annual turnover of at least £100,000 with a projected growth to, say, a minimum of £200,000 within a year or so. Companies with a smaller turnover than this would not generate enough business to make it worthwhile for the factor.

Supposing a company has sales of £200,000 a year and allows about seventy days' credit to its customers. There will, therefore, at any given time be about £40,000 owing to the company. The factor might have agreed to provide 80 per cent of the invoice value up-front – say, £32,000. The company may use up to 80 per cent of the value of its trade debts, on which it might be charged interest at, for example, 3 per cent over base rate. It would also pay a fee of about 2 per cent of gross turnover for the factor's accounting, collection and bad debt protection services. The service fee varies from as little as 0.75 per cent in some cases to as much as 3 per cent in others; the exact fee depends on the volume of sales involved and the spread and type of debtors.

Types of factoring   There are three types of factoring: non-recourse, where the factor provides bad debt protection (favoured by the larger companies where there is an element of credit risk among their customers); recourse, where the factor has recourse to the client for bad debts (used mainly by smaller companies); and invoice discounting, which is basically factoring without the service element (used mainly by companies with sales in excess of £1 million, which have a well-organised and efficient sales accounting and credit control function).

Invoice discounting   With invoice discounting, the company simply gets a pre-payment on its invoices, less a discount, from the factor but does not use any of the ancillary services. The company itself sends out the invoices to its customers, runs the sales ledger and collects payments. At no point will the customer come into contact with, or know about, the factor. The advantages of invoice discounting are that it is cheaper than factoring and it is confidential, since the company maintains direct contact with its customers. However, companies discounting usually have to bear the cost of any bad debts.

From the factor's point of view, invoice discounting is riskier, because the factor has to rely on the company to collect payment instead of on its own staff. For this reason, it is generally not available to companies with turnovers of less than £1 million a year. Finance advanced is charged at overdraft rate, and there is an administrative fee for the service of between 0.2 per cent and 0.7 per cent of sales.

Use in the Community

Factoring exists in most member states to varying degrees. It is widely used in Italy and West Germany. The services provided are much the same as those provided in the UK. After 1992, there may well be some cross-border competition from factoring companies in various member states, but this is not expected to affect the market place significantly as regards UK business, at least in the short term. As more small and medium-sized companies start to export to the EC, there is likely to be a marked expansion in the volume of business done by factoring companies, because companies that find it difficult handling trade customers at home are bound to find it even more troublesome where foreign languages, culture and currencies are involved.

The mechanics of factoring are the same, irrespective of whether domestic or foreign trade is involved. For instance, the factor's approval is required before credit cover can be granted to any customer, whether UK or European. Once the terms of business are approved, the normal factoring service is provided. Where a company invoices in the currency of the country it is trading with, factoring

Currency risk

provides an in-built protection against currency risk – the risk of seeing profits eroded by a fall, during the credit period, in the value of the foreign currency in relation to sterling.

The larger UK companies already trading in the EC will be used to handling currency risk and hedging, as appropriate. It is the smaller business, trading for the first time in unfamiliar markets, that may find factoring a useful mechanism to minimise risk of loss through bad debts and currency movements. If a UK business wishes to use factoring primarily for its EC business, any shortfall of the minimum turnover criterion can be made up by putting part of its UK business through the factor as well.

The route to factoring in either the UK or in the EC lies through your local bank manager or, if you wish to shop around and see what the market has to offer, through the Association of British Factors.

This body represents the ten major players in the factoring market and between them they handle a volume of business valued at nearly £8.8 billion in 1988. In that period, the companies in the Association served the interests of 6,180 clients, the majority of whom were in the manufacturing, distribution or service industries.

Forfaiting

Forfaiting may be unfamiliar to many UK companies but, by 1992, many more will be using it for their sales into the EC. It provides them with a risk-free way of extending credit to customers while receiving cash on shipment themselves. As a purely free-market technique that works best in relatively stable countries, its importance compared with finance backed by export credit agency has grown. It is a common technique among Italian and West German companies and is likely to become as common in the UK. (See pp. 126–7 for a case study on how Bayswater Tubes and Sections uses forfaiting.)

Despite its strange name, forfaiting is a simple concept: without recourse discounting. You receive a series of promissory notes or accepted bills of exchange from the buyer and sell them immediately for cash to a forfaiter. The forfaiter takes the risk (the forfaiter *forfeits* the right to come back to you if the buyer does not pay) and you get the money.

As short-term forfaiting has become more popular, its effect from the trader's point of view has become more and more like factoring. The key differences are that factoring can provide a complete sales ledger service, while forfaiting is just a very efficient form of financing; and that factoring usually provides up to 80 per cent finance, while forfaiting gives 100 per cent.

The origins of forfaiting lie in the 1950s when exporters in West Germany wanted to sell to Eastern Europe. The basic goods were capital equipment and the regular credit terms were five years. West German companies received promissory notes or bills of exchange, payable every six months, and guaranteed by a bank in the importing country. The exporter then sold the notes to a forfaiter, usually Swiss in those days, who would calculate the present value of the notes and give the discounted cash sum to the exporter. The technique suited the German way of business. The credit was effectively fixed rate, the company bore no credit risk and the cash balances were steadily built up. Italian companies liked it too and soon they were the second biggest users of forfaiting after the West Germans.

Ten-by-six

This sort of forfaiting is usually called the 'classic' à forfait or 'ten-by-six' (ten equal promissory notes payable at six-month intervals

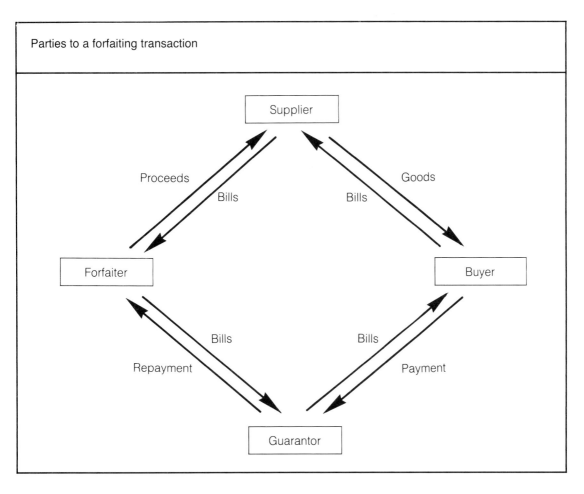

Parties to a forfaiting transaction

over the five-year credit term). But the development of forfaiting, due largely to the arrival of London banks and specialist forfaiting houses in the market, has meant that almost anything can now be financed through the market: ninety-day terms for consumer goods, say, or military equiment over a few years, up to huge thirteen-year projects. Short-term forfaiting often substitutes deferred payment letters of credit for promissory notes. Cigarettes, plumbing equipment, even footballers, have been forfaited over the last couple of years. Generally, forfaiting covers deals worth more than £50,000, although smaller, repeat business could also be covered.

How does forfaiting work?

Because of the way the technique has developed there is really no typical forfaiting transaction these days. The fastest growing area of the business is probably short-term trade – credit periods of up to 360 days. But the classic ten-by-six illustrates the main features and gives a guide to organising a deal. The principles of forfaiting remain the same whatever the size of the deal, the type of goods, the buyer and seller or the length of the credit term.

First, speak to a forfaiter as soon as you think there is a chance of closing the deal. All the major banks have forfaiting units or subsidiaries and there are also some independent houses that are very active in the business. Getting some preliminary advice from them will help you when it comes to negotiating the sales finance. If the deal looks certain, ask the forfaiter for a commitment. He will charge a fee for this but you will have the certainty that the price he quotes will be the actual price for the deal. The fee will be expressed annually (1 per cent) or on a monthly basis (about 0.1 per cent). Forfaiters claim to be able to give an immediate response for straightforward cases or will call back within the hour for a more complicated transaction. The verbal commitment is backed up by written confirmation.

Charging

The forfaiter will guide you on how much to charge your customer. The total will equal the sales price plus interest charges over the credit period, plus an amount that reflects the risk that the money will not be paid when the notes mature. As the promissory notes (or bills of exchange) are usually guaranteed by a first-class bank in the importer's country, this margin in effect represents the risk of national upheaval. The net result is, though, that you can tell your customer exactly what interest charge you are passing on: the finance is, by definition, fixed rate.

When the sales contract is signed and a delivery date agreed, the forfaiter can move ahead with the technical details of the transaction. He needs evidence of debt; in the case of a ten-by-six, ten promissory notes maturing at six-month intervals for the next five years. The paper will also include a guarantee from a bank in the buyer's country. This may be a separate piece of paper, guaranteeing that the buyer's obligation will be assumed by the bank, or an *aval* (in French and German, or *avallo* in Italian), which is simply written on the document.

Aval

Recourse

The actual details of the sale are completely independent of the financing because forfaiting provides finance without any recourse to the exporter. But usually, the evidence of debt will be presented at about the same time as the delivery of goods. The forfaiter buys the notes or bills for cash and will then hold them for presentation as they become due or, if he wants, sell them to an investing institution or another forfaiter in the secondary market.

It is worth noting that forfait rates are usually expressed as discount rates, rather than interest rates; this is because the amount

Who pays the financing costs? Example of a forfaiting transaction

Normally the finance costs of the transaction are passed on to the client's counter party, e.g. the buyer, since it is he who is obtaining the benefit of credit. This is achieved by incorporating the interest and days of grace, together with the contract price, into the bills of exchange/promissory notes.

The following example illustrates how this is achieved:

Basic data:
Required amount: US$1,000,000
Credit term: 5 years from shipment
Contract date: May 1988
Shipment date: November 1988
Repayment: 10 semi-annual bills
Days of grace: 2
Commitment period: 6 months
Commitment fee: 1% pa

Structure
Purchase date: November 1988
*Full amount of net proceeds before deduction of the commitment fee.

Maturity dates	Principal amount	Bill amount (incl. interest)	Net proceeds
May 1989	US$100,000	US$151,236	US$144,059
November 1989	100,000	146,113	132,535
May 1990	100,000	140,989	121,885
November 1990	100,000	135,866	111,849
May 1991	100,000	130,742	102,579
November 1991	100,000	125,618	93,803
May 1992	100,000	120,495	85,731
November 1992	100,000	115,371	78,209
May 1993	100,000	110,247	71,189
November 1993	100,000	105,124	64,677
	US$1,000,000	US$1,281,801	US$1,006,516*

Interest cost: 9.801435% pa
Discount rate: 8.175343% pa

Fee calculation: 1% pa on face value of bills

$$US\$1,281,801 \times \frac{1}{100} \times \frac{183}{360} = US\$6,516$$

Net Proceeds: US$1,006,516 less US$6,516 = US$1,000,000

NB. It may well be that bills of exchange etc. are in existence without prior discussions with the Forfaiting Unit. In such circumstances purchase can be achieved. However such purchase would be normally at a discount and as a result finance costs would be for the account of the beneficiary of payment, if such costs had not been incorporated already in the contract price.

that the exporter receives is calculated by discounting interest and risk margin from the total amount the importer pays.

A great advantage of forfaiting is that it makes any sale abroad just as easy as a domestic cash sale. The exporter may want £500,000 for a shipment to a German customer who wants to pay in Deutschemarks over five years. The forfaiter will handle all the calculations and pay cash in sterling upon delivery of the promissory notes. The exporter can be safe in the knowledge that, financially, an unknown company hundreds of miles away is no longer its customer – a high street bank, with assets of billions of pounds is responsible for payment.

Credit Reference

Defaults

Particularly when selling on open account, it is essential to carry out credit checks on your customers. In the UK alone, about 13,000 businesses foundered in 1988, many of them contributing to the failure of others to whom they owed money. Even more importantly, businesses must remember to carry out regular checks on overseas, including EC, customers. This is no more than good practice for management of the debtor book. You may start off cautiously, but can easily become complacent as payments roll in on time – until one day, they just stop.

Traditional methods

Bank references

Fortunately, it has become much easier in the last few years to obtain good status reports on companies in the EC, thanks to the development of computerised information exchanges. These should be used to supplement the traditional form of credit checking (bank and trade references). If an overseas branch of your UK bank knows your customer, a bank reference is valuable. But if you have to rely on an unconnected bank (which your own bank will contact for you), you may find it unwilling to be uncomplimentary about its customer. That said, Continental bank references do tend to be more comprehensive than those given in the UK.

Trade references

Trade references – those that are given by other suppliers named by your customer – can be misleading, as your customer will always have a few valuable suppliers he wants to keep happy by paying on time. The problem of straight fraud is also a serious one. Documents can be forged, or trade references can come from companies that are secretly controlled by your potential customer. The lesson here is 'Seller Beware!'

The computer revolution

The most reliable method is to have someone on the ground. Your local agent may be the answer, if you are certain he will not be over-optimistic because he values his commission. An alternative is to use a local credit-checking agency, which should have the best information of all. There are now computer link-ups between agencies across the world providing standardised data on companies. This includes balance-sheet information, history, who the directors are and so on, but may also include the company's payment performance, whether that is getting better or worse, and even how it compares with the industry average. You can get these reports sent to you on paper, or you may be able to look at them, via a telephone line, on your own microcomputer. The world's biggest credit-checking company, which gathers information from its own offices, has even developed a system that allows you to use an ordinary telephone as a computer terminal. Your bank will be able to advise on where to go for the best credit data. It is not worth being caught out when the information is now so easy to obtain.

5. Alternative short-term borrowing techniques

Chapters 5 and 6 deal with more sophisticated and ordinarily larger-scale borrowing facilities which might be available to larger corporate borrowers to meet their particular needs. Such financing methods may not relate directly to the needs of the customer expanding into the EC but are outlined for illustrative purposes; banks like to treat their customers individually, tailoring borrowing facilities to their individual needs. The most appropriate funding methods will be determined by the corporate customer's own circumstances, preferences and, naturally, strategies for the future.

In addition to short-term finance specifically related to trade (as detailed in the previous chapter), there are other short-term borrowing facilities available to companies. Short-term loans (normally anything for repayment within a year) are the most flexible, in that they can be more easily tailored to seasonal or other cyclical requirements. Medium-term (say up to ten years) and long-term loans might be negotiated to reflect other needs.

Maturity   The choice of maturity will very much reflect your expectation of future cash-flow. The maturity, that is, the end of the bank's agreement to lend on the terms negotiated at the outset, will ordinarily be geared to expected ability to repay at that time.

Additionally, the corporate treasurer will need to decide whether to go for floating- or fixed-rate loans, and what currencies should be borrowed. During the period of a loan, in most cases, the final rate of interest is not fixed; it varies according to market rates, often calculated as a fixed percentage above LIBOR (London Interbank Offered Rate). For administrative ease, however, the rate is usually fixed for short periods of say one or three months (the fixture period), subject to revision at the market rate at the end of the fixture period. The rate is therefore variable but fixed in the short term.

As an alternative the corporate treasurer may decide to avoid the risk of having to bear higher interest costs than expected at the outset by fixing the interest rate throughout the life of the loan, that is, until its maturity. Most banks will discuss fixed interest advances with their corporate customers but it should be borne in mind that fixed interest rates will always be higher than the variable market rates at the time of negotiation because of the rate exposure the bank will be carrying.

Short-term LIBOR-linked loans

In the domestic sterling interbank market, medium and large corporate customers can get competitive borrowing rates where the interest payable is based on a margin over LIBOR. Such loans are flexible and can range from one month to twelve months. Negotiations can be undertaken direct with a bank or through a money broker. Ordinarily such borrowings do not come with a commitment from the bank except to the extent that it will continue to lend provided it remains satisfied with the creditworthiness of the customer.

Acceptance credits

There is an established market for bills of exchange drawn by customers on their bankers, under facilities agreed between them, to finance specific areas of their trade. This would be regarded as part of a corporate customer's working finance facilities, since the bank would be 'on risk' during the currency of the bill, which it accepts as payable at a maturity date perhaps one or three months in the future. Carrying the bank's acceptance (for which a commission is payable), the bill can be discounted at fine rates in the market to provide the customer with relatively cheap, short-term uncommitted finance.

DAB   A refinement of this is the Direct Acceptance Bid (DAB) under which the treasurer of a very large corporate might invite the treasurers of a number of banks to bid for bills of exchange he proposes to draw. Taking up the bids of the most competitive banks, the corporation minimises the cost of the short-term finance being raised.

Market line

Many large corporate borrowers have access direct to the dealing rooms of the banks and are able to draw short-term money at highly competitive market rates on a very informal basis. Customers' access to such funds is always strictly at the bank's option and there is no commitment to lend at any particular rate or, indeed, to lend at all if at the time it does not suit the bank's position in the market.

Short-term Eurocurrency loans

These are useful for protecting against exchange rate changes. If a UK exporter is due to receive a payment in French francs in six months' time, but is worried that the franc will depreciate against the pound in the meantime, the exporter could borrow an equivalent amount in francs in the Euromoney market and exchange it for sterling, thus receiving the funds immediately. If the franc depreciates, the exporter does not suffer an exchange rate loss. The Eurocurrency loan is paid off when the francs are received in six months' time. Most loans in the Eurocurrency market are linked to LIBOR, and maturities available range from overnight to twelve months.

Commercial paper

Sterling commercial paper (CP) has grown rapidly in popularity among corporate treasurers as an effective method of raising short-term finance direct from investors. The UK CP market was established only in 1986, when the Budget made it permissible. The concept comes from the USA, where for more than a century it has been a source of short-term funding.

CP is unsecured short-term promissory bearer notes, issued by large companies to investors in notes of £100,000, £500,000 or £1,000,000. Maturities can be from seven to 364 days. In the UK, issuers have to be listed on the International Stock Exchange (London), or on the Unlisted Securities Market, or be approved by the ISE. They must have a net worth above £25 million. The growth in the use of CP is an example of the trend towards 'disintermediation' whereby companies borrow money direct from investors, not through the banks as intermediaries. However, the banks are usually involved, since it is they who will generally sell the paper to the investors on behalf of the issuers.

Advantages Among its advantages are that effective interest rates are competitive compared with other borrowing methods (pricing is related to LIBOR), maturities are flexible, funds can be raised quickly, and issuing and operating costs are low. A drawback is that an issuer has access to funds only if there are enough willing investors – issues are not underwritten to guarantee a successful take-up. This means that in order to launch a successful CP programme the issuer must be well known to the investors it is seeking to attract. However, any responsible dealing bank will be able to evaluate quickly and efficiently the likely investor acceptance of a given programme, and prevent the unfortunate possibility of the paper not being absorbed by the market.

The potential CP issuer should remember that it will be rubbing shoulders in the market with companies such as Sainsbury, BP and Next. Over half the companies listed in the FT-SE 100 Index have established sterling CP facilities.

ECP
The Eurocommercial paper (ECP) market, with more than 700 issuers and with outstandings of around $100 billion, is far bigger than the sterling CP market. Its importance is expected to grow rather than diminish. In addition to those in the UK, there are already markets in France and the Netherlands, while the deregulation of some EC financial markets, particularly Italy, should provide a fillip to the ECP programme.

6.   Medium- and long-term borrowing

Companies that need to borrow for periods of a year or more have a variety of medium- and long-term facilities to choose from. As with the short-term financing techniques outlined in the previous chapter, such medium- and long-term finance may not relate directly to the need of companies expanding into the EC, but may be needed as part of an overall business strategy. As with short-term finance, the corporate treasurer will have to decide whether to opt for floating- or fixed-rate finance, and in what currencies to borrow.

Medium-term LIBOR-linked loans

These are usually negotiated for purchases of machinery, property and other fixed capital needs; they can be made available for 'general' corporate purposes too, but usually only to large and well-established borrowers. The bank is committed to lend for a set term at an interest rate calculated at a fixed margin over LIBOR (whereas an overdraft would normally be linked to the bank's base rate). They are therefore floating interest-rate loans, the rate periodically varying as LIBOR varies, although in practice it will be fixed for short periods (say one or three months) – the administrative burden of a daily calculation would be too great. The margin will vary according to the status of the borrower, the purpose of the advance etc., in fact the lender's perception of risk.

Terms   Typically, the minimum amount will be around £250,000, with no maximum. Normally ten years will be the maximum term, although it can be as long as fifteen years. Repayments are usually by periodic instalments over the life of the loan, although a single 'bullet' repayment at maturity can be agreed if circumstances are right. Repayment holidays can be included at the early stages of the loan, which can be useful if there is a time lag between taking out the loan and income being generated by the project or purpose for which the loan was required. The precise terms of the repayment to which a potential lender will be most agreeable will be affected by the

Definition	Medium-term LIBOR-linked loans	Fixed-term loan scheme	Multiple option facilities (MOFs)
	A loan facility 'committed' as to availability of funds over a medium term and with interest calculated at a fixed margin over LIBOR	A committed loan facility with an interest rate fixed at the outset for the full term of the loan	A flexible facility with a range of funding alternatives tailored to suit customer's specific needs An MOF incorporates an uncommitted short-term finance facility at money market rates and a committed medium-term facility A range of financial institutions are involved both short-term and long-term with a bank acting as agent Uncommitted short-term finance will vary from corporate to corporate depending upon requirements but separate tender panels may be put in place to cover drawings by way of: Cash advances (sterling/currency) Acceptance credits Sterling commercial paper Committed medium-term finance: requirements will vary but normally include: Cash advances (sterling/currency) Acceptance credits At an agreed floating-rate margin for a specified period

Availability	All categories of customers but normally corporates	All customers with a fixed term requirement, but normally corporates	Corporate customers
Purpose	Usually for specific projects but may be for revolving 'working capital' facilities	Ideally for specific products or to re-finance existing facilities	Working capital, including re-financing of existing credit lines, may include back-up line for sterling commercial paper
Customer benefit	A committed facility Flexible source of medium-term finance Access to money market related interest rates With a repayment holiday – ability to finance a new production facility which may take some years to achieve full output and profitability	Cost of finance fixed at outset Competitively rated Bullet/amortising repayment	Finest short-term market rates Medium-term commitment Little administration required Simplicity of raising funds Easy access to a range of options Advantage of comparative rates Retain relationships with banks
Amount	Minimum £250,000 No maximum	Minimum £250,000 Maximum £10,000,000	Minimum £20,000,000 No maximum

continued overleaf

	Medium-term LIBOR-linked loans	Fixed-term loan scheme	Multiple option facilities (MOFs)
Term	Normally up to 10 years (but up to 15 years may be considered) Repayments will usually be by periodic instalments Repayment holidays can be included Bullet repayment can be arranged	Minimum 2 years Maximum 10 years	Normally 3–10 years Drawings under the tender panels are usually for short periods
Interest rate	The rate will reflect the financial standing of the customer and the term of the loan and may be stepped (i.e. an increasing interest rate over the term of the loan) Linked to LIBOR plus MLAs No interest set-off arrangements are available	The rate will reflect the financial standing of the customer and the term of the loan No interest set-off arrangements are available The rate is inclusive of MLAs	Uncommitted short term: banks bid at a margin over LIBOR plus MLAs Medium-term commitment: at an agreed margin over LIBOR plus MLAs No interest set-off arrangements available The rates offered will reflect the financial standing of the customer
Fees	An arrangement fee to cover the bank's up-front costs would be normal A commitment fee would be normal	An arrangement fee to cover the bank's up-front costs would be normal	A front-end fee to the lead/agent bank An annual underwriting/commitment fee for the bank's providing the medium-term commitment

	A fee may be levied for early repayment Non-utilisation fees would normally be sought		A utilisation fee if the committed facility is used An annual agency fee payable to the lead/agent bank for administrative responsibilities
Documentation	A facility letter is required	A facility letter is required	A facility agreement is always required – normally prepared by solicitors
Security	Normal banking considerations will apply	Normal banking considerations will apply	Normal banking considerations will apply

Fees

customer's evidenced ability to repay in the future. Quite apart from interest on the loan, fees will be payable to cover the bank's administrative costs and also to reflect its commitment to lend until maturity. Fees will usually consist of an arrangement fee to cover the bank's up-front costs; a commitment fee; a penalty fee for early repayment; and, when applicable, a non-utilisation fee. Security may be required if a large loan is syndicated (i.e. managed through one bank but with funds lent by a syndicate of banks). A management fee will usually also be payable in the case of syndicated loans.

Fixed-term loans

These loans have an interest rate fixed at the outset for the full term. The rates are not linked to LIBOR, but reflect the financial standing of the customer and the term of the loan. They can be used for similar purposes to LIBOR-linked loans, and although the same minimum of £250,000 normally applies, the maximum might be £10 million from any one source. The term is usually between two and ten years and security may be required. There would be an arrangement fee at the outset.

Syndicated loans in the Euromarkets

These are medium- or long-term loans for large amounts in Eurocurrencies where banks group together to provide the facilities. They are based on the interest rates linked to LIBOR. The advantage to the large corporate customer is that large sums, perhaps several hundred million dollars, can be raised quickly. With the international debt crisis in the mid-1980s, banks became less willing to tie up so much money in this way. As a result, for large sums the banks started to explore alternative forms of lending and began to act as arrangers of finance rather than as providers. This has led to growth in the issuing of short-term Euronotes and long-term Eurobonds.

However, in the late 1980s syndicated loans – also known as participating loans – came back into favour. In 1987, for example, turnover exceeded $80 billion (albeit concentrated in a few large banks) and the customer base has widened beyond sovereign states and into the corporate sector.

Advantages

Corporate treasurers have found that with syndicated loans they can influence their debt profile more effectively than if they issue bonds, which quickly dissolve into the secondary market. Other attractions of the loan market over the capital debt market are that it remains open to borrowers in bad times as well as good; it will accommodate the less than Triple-A-rated company, and offer entry to the new-comer lacking an international credit record; its structures are relatively flexible and more easily shaped to suit the customer than are those of the bond market, where uniformity is a necessity; and the participating market has proved able to raise large amounts of money very quickly. Treasurers have also found that by careful pricing and by choosing the lead bank with care, they can gain contact with banks likely to help with other matters, such as export financing, currency problems and the like.

UK and other EC banks have always enjoyed massive placing power, and syndicated loans could play an important role in the post-1992 financing competition. In particular, they could be an important method of financing leveraged buy-outs (LBOs) – the US takeover mechanism which is now spreading rapidly into the EC.

Euronotes

Euronotes are short-term bearer negotiable paper sold by companies to investors in the Euromarkets. The banks (which act as arrangers) have developed various facilities to allow these notes to be issued on a revolving basis over several years, so creating medium-term finance at short-term rates. The notes are tradeable, the resulting liquidity making them more attractive to investors than loans, and making it easier and cheaper for borrowers to raise large sums. Denominations are in large amounts, such as $250,000 or $1 million and for maturities of usually one to six months. The notes either pay interest or are issued at discount.

Interest rates   From a corporate treasurer's point of view, they are a cheap form of medium-term finance at times when short-term interest rates are more attractive. As soon as the interest rate position reverses and medium-term rates become more favourable, the treasurer can simply stop issuing notes and switch to a different method of financing.

Euronote terminology can become confusing, because the banks offer various back-stop facilities which guarantee that the borrower can raise its finance at any given time. In the event that there is no demand for the notes in the market, the banks will usually (at a price) have underwritten the facility and be committed to lending to the borrower in some other form. They charge fees for these underwriting facilities. Banks are usually engaged at the outset to sell the notes to investors in the markets and an extra fee for the service will be charged.

Medium-term notes

One of the more recent innovations in fixed-term finance is the emergence of medium-term notes. Like their first cousin, commercial paper, medium-term notes (MTNs) have been imported from the USA, where they have been widely accepted and where their number has grown rapidly to over fifty billion dollars' worth of notes outstanding by the middle of 1988. In the EC only a small fraction of this is outstanding, but the market is growing fast and, like all new debt instruments, their successful absorption by the market demands time for issuers and investors alike to develop an understanding of their advantages and disadvantages.

MTNs are a hybrid instrument – a sort of cross between short-term CP and longer-dated bonds. So closely related are MTNs to CP that an alternative name for them could almost be 'longer-term commercial paper'.

MTNs are issued at fixed interest rates and generally carry maturities of between one and five years, although programmes of up to ten years have been known ('medium' is fairly loosely defined). One of the most important characteristics that these instruments share with CP is that they are offered on a continuous basis, giving the corporate treasurer flexibility in managing regular borrowing requirements for funds up to, say, three to five years.

Issue As with CP, MTNs are issued either through a placement agency, a tender panel, or, most commonly, through appointed dealers. To ensure diversification (from the issuer's perspective) and to reduce risk (from the dealer's), there will generally be more than one dealer, and a syndicate will be formed which will then sell the notes on to investors on a best effort basis. Dealers, usually large investment banks with extensive access to international investors, then undertake to make markets in the notes, theoretically ensuring a smooth and active secondary market. This is important for issuers because the more widely the notes are distributed, the more widely the issuer's name as a good and stable borrower becomes known. Fees are payable to dealers.

Also like CP, the notes are not underwritten, because they are in a bond issue or equity placement.

Compound facilities

MOF

It has become common for the large borrower to negotiate a multi-option facility (MOF) to meet funding needs. Ordinarily this will contain uncommitted and committed elements: the uncommitted being, perhaps, acceptances under which the treasurers of a panel of banks are invited to bid competitively for bills, or Euronotes; the committed being a revolving underwriting facility (RUF). The RUF is a more expensive back-stop facility if, for any reason, the cheaper short-term options are unavailable.

The benefit of an MOF to the customer is that it provides maximum flexibility, highly competitive funding and the comfort of the bankers' commitment to lend, all in a single package negotiated through one lead bank.

Long-term borrowing

Debentures

The chief long-term financing options for large corporates in the domestic market are debentures and convertible loan stock. Debentures are bonds paying a fixed rate of interest to the holder. They may be secured on the fixed assets of the company and might have a life of twenty or twenty-five years, or longer.

Convertible loan stock

Convertible loan stock is not secured on company assets, and at some stage in its life may be converted into shares of the company. Such stock will have long maturities and pay fixed interest.

Foreign bond issue

The company could also seek to raise off-shore funds through a foreign bond issue, which can be done in domestic markets or the Eurobond market. Eurobonds (see pp. 120–22) are generally sold on behalf of companies by international syndicates of banks. They can be sold to investors in many countries and are usually issued in stable and fully convertible currencies; the dollar is the most popular. Eurobonds are normally fixed interest, but they can be floating rate (known as floating-rate notes, or floating-rate bonds).

7. Interest-rate risk management

Whatever types of borrowing a company opts for, it may be necessary to guard against fluctuations in interest rates and exchange rates. Floating interest rates and exchange rates can damage your company's health and very few companies, large or small, can afford to ignore them. Volatile foreign exchange markets can wipe out profits overnight and remove a company's competitive edge in a key export market in the same short time, exposing it to damaging losses. Movements in interest rates can be equally damaging.

The need for companies to protect themselves from the volatile financial markets has grown as governments have used fiscal monetary policies to curb inflation. In the UK industry has, in addition, been under strong pressure to export and this in itself has led to increased exposure to adverse movements in interest rates, as companies borrow to expand capacity. With the onset of 1992 this pressure will intensify. Smaller companies tend to be particularly at risk since many lack the financial resources and expertise of the large, multinational groups, but larger companies are by no means immune from the problems. UK companies are, in the main, well practised in protecting themselves against turbulence in the foreign exchange markets (see pp. 85–8), but treasury consultants point out they have been slower to identify the risks in the area of interest rates.

A company must be clear as to its needs, since selecting the wrong hedging tool can be as damaging as not bothering to use one at all. It must bear in mind the flexibility it will require from the deal and the cost of the hedge in relation to the risk faced.

The forward-rate agreement

The forward-rate agreement (FRA) is relatively new, in that it has been in existence only since 1983, but it has developed rapidly since then. The FRA is basically a contract to pay or receive an agreed fixed rate of interest for a forward period. It must be emphasised that the agreement covers only the interest-rate element and does not commit

Forward agreement

the bank to lend or the customer to borrow. There is no obligation to make a loan or deposit. The agreement is based on a notional sum – unlike a forward agreement, where a real sum is involved – so that a company can gain protection without using up valuable credit lines.

The agreement, therefore, allows companies which are borrowing for fixed periods to cover themselves against adverse interest rate movements by locking in borrowing costs. The FRA is available in a range of major currencies (including the increasingly popular ecu) and within a wide range of fixed amounts. This makes for flexibility.

One bank, for instance, offers FRA contracts for $2 million to $30 million and for 1 billion yen to 5 billion yen. However, it is possible to secure contracts for much smaller amounts, such as $100,000, and it is the availability of deals at the smaller end of the contract range which is leading to an increased use of the FRA by middle-sized companies.

How does a company go about setting up an FRA with its bank? Suppose Bloggins PLC finds at the beginning of the calendar year that it will have to borrow $2 million for a three-month period beginning 1 April, and the company treasurer, having looked into his crystal ball, wishes to protect the company's coffers against a future rise in interest rates. The company might, therefore, decide to buy an FRA. The company approaches its bankers and asks for a price for an FRA for the relevant sum and period. The bank quotes a rate of, say, 10 per cent on the $2 million sum for a three-month period. Remember, the cash sum on which the deal is based is notional and does not form an obligation to make or take delivery of the amount specified.

Two days before the start of the contract period the contract rate (10 per cent in this case) is compared with actual market LIBOR for three month dollars, commencing 1 April. The latter rate is called the settlement rate and the difference between this rate and the contract is settled by a net cash payment on the day the contract is due to start.

If at maturity the treasurer has proved to be correct and interest rates have risen, then the company will receive a payment from the bank. For instance, if interest rates had risen to 11 per cent, then the bank would have to pay the company 1 per cent on $2m – the difference between the settlement and contract rates, in this case – for a three-month period. The interest rate is discounted to present value because the settlement payment has been made at the start of the period. If, however, the treasurer is proved wrong and interest rates have fallen, then the company will have to pay the bank the difference between the two rates. This transaction will be offset, however, by a reduction in the interest paid on the actual money which Bloggins PLC has borrowed.

The introduction of new or hybrid instruments is normally market-driven in that they are created to solve a particular problem. A large company involved in an overseas takeover would, for example, use a wide range of financial tools, including FRAs to hedge against risks.

Interest-rate futures

The FRA, which benefits from a market with considerable depth and in which fine spreads are available, has several advantages over interest-rate futures, which are, theoretically, another solution to the interest-rate problem. A futures contract is basically an agreement to make or take delivery of a specified interest rate commitment on an agreed future date at a price specified when the deal is struck.

Futures contracts come only in set nominal amounts; a small percentage, called a margin, has to be deposited. Futures contracts are traded on exchanges such as the London International Financial Futures Exchange (LIFFE). A rise in interest rates causes futures prices to fall, and a fall in interest rates causes futures prices to rise. So, a company that is worried that interest rates might rise could sell interest-rate futures. Any increase in rates would cause futures prices to fall, and if the company had sold futures it would make money on the difference between the price it agreed to sell and the price the futures had actually fallen to. If interest rates had fallen, the company would have lost on the futures but it would have gained by having lower borrowing costs.

Interest-rate futures are flexible, but require much more monitoring than FRAs, a factor which puts many corporate treasurers off and means that they tend to be used mainly by banks and other financial institutions. The futures market is still essentially limited in the range of contracts it offers. In addition, the FRA avoids the accounting and margin problems encountered with a futures transaction, and it is more flexible. Contract dates, for example, are available for around two years, and longer if necessary, while the interest-rate futures market is locked into specified trading periods.

Interest-rate options

An interest-rate option is another protection against adverse fluctuations. An option gives the buyer (holder) the right, but not the obligation, to receive or pay on a set date a fixed sum at an agreed rate. It is basically a form of insurance policy, for which the buyer pays a

LIFFE

premium to the seller of the option (the bank). The sum involved in an option is notional. The contract applies only to interest rates, and the underlying loan on which the contract is taken out is not affected by the agreement.

Options can be used both by a borrower, such as a company which is expanding or has taken out a loan to cover a seasonal fall in cash flow, and an investor.

Interest-rate options appeared in the early 1980s. Insurance companies were the prime movers, but they eventually concluded that options did not fit into their business activities, as a result of which the banks took up the baton. The use of options has since spread from the USA and although they are still largely dollar denominated, European and Far Eastern banks have been busily developing them to take in a growing number of currencies, including sterling, the yen and the Australian dollar.

There are variations on the options theme, called caps, floors and collars. This trinity of interest-rate options encompasses a range of sophisticated financing which enables companies to hedge against adverse movements in rates by limiting rates from moving above or below certain levels. Because of their sophistication, caps, collars and floors are in general more appealing to the bigger players. But they are also more expensive than forward-rate agreements, which has made some smaller companies wary of using them.

Caps

Caps are used by borrowers to put a 'cap' on how high interest rates can rise. They are aimed primarily at giving the company with rolling floating-rate borrowings insurance against an increase in interest rates above a specified level. One of their chief advantages is that, while affording a company protection against interest-rate increases, they also enable it to take advantage of a fall in rates which will automatically apply to the actual loan taken out by the company.

An interest-rate cap is normally geared to the key three- or six-month LIBOR, which would then be compared to the cap rate on each of the settlement dates (every three months in a deal based on the three-month LIBOR, for example). If the LIBOR selected is higher than the cap rate on settlement date, the company (the buyer) would be compensated for the value of the difference, but if the selected LIBOR is lower than the cap rate, no payment will be made to the company. Nevertheless, it will benefit from the lower interest rate on the underlying loan.

Take Bloggins PLC, which has negotiated an $8 million loan to pay for expansion. The loan is on a floating-rate basis, linked to the three-month LIBOR. The treasurer, however, feels that interest rates will rise and decides to buy a cap at 7 per cent for two years, again based on the three-month LIBOR, and pays a premium to the bank for the facility. Bloggins proves correct and interest rates rise to 9 per cent. In this case the bank will have to compensate the company for the value of the difference in the rates, that is, 2 per cent.

The rates will be checked thereafter every three months, because the company has based its borrowing on the three-month LIBOR, and if during that time interest rates should fall below the cap, then obviously the company would receive no further compensation. The device is neat. It is flexible because a company need not hang on to an option until the bitter end, which could be seven years or more. The option or cap can be sold to the bank, based on its value at the time, so the buyer can recoup some of its costs. But the company usually has to be prepared to pay the fee at the outset, and there is the rub for some company treasurers. The method of calculating that cost is complicated, and the banks have employed computer models to determine the various elements which contribute to the price of the contract. One of the key elements which will have to be examined is the time at which the contract expires. Obviously the longer the contract is set to last the greater the likelihood of an option being exercised.

This leads to another element of pricing – that of volatility. If markets are volatile, or look like becoming so, you will have to pay more. But, of course, the bank will have to consider the interest rate at which the option will be exercised, which is known as the strike price. When considering this element the bank must also look at the previous level of interest rates and the gap between that level and the strike price. If, for instance, interest rates are standing at 10 per cent when the deal is made and the strike price is 11 per cent, the option is much more likely to be exercised than if there were larger gaps between the two rates. Therefore, the narrower the gap, the higher the cost. Another factor the bank has to include in its calculations is the rate at which the premium can be invested.

When all these variables have been determined a contract price is set, and it is the price that has deterred many a company from using caps. But banks emphasise that these instruments provide a flexible form of insurance and enable a company to keep a grip on insurance costs.

Floors

The procedures used to set up and calculate a cap also apply to the interest-rate floor agreement, which basically performs the opposite task to a cap. Under an interest-rate floor contract, the seller (the bank) agrees to pay the investor or buyer compensation based on the interest-rate differential created if rates fall below a specified level over an agreed period. If the rate, again usually based on the three-month or six-month LIBOR, is above the agreed floor, then no payment is made. The obvious advantages of using such an agreement are that an investor is assured a minimum return while still being able to reap the benefits of a rise in interest rates on the underlying loan.

Short-term hedging techniques			
	Forward-rate agreements	Financial futures	Interest-rate guarantees (options)
Currencies	US$, £, DM, SFr, yen, ecu, Fr	US$, £, yen	Major market in US$. Limited availability in £, DM and yen
Amounts	Min.: US$1m (or eq.). Max.: no preset maximum	Standardised contract sizes (e.g. Euro-dollars, US$1m)	Min.: US$3m (or eq.)
Price quotations	Close prices in active traded periods	Very close prices in nearby contract months, prices wider in distant contract months	A single premium quoted for transactions required by customer. (A two-way price would be wider than FRAs.)
Flexibility	Amounts and periods tailored to customer needs	Standardised contract specifications	Amounts and periods tailored to customer needs
Impact of interest-rate changes	Rate fixed	Rate fixed	Protected from unfavourable movement but ability to benefit from favourable movement
Reversal of transaction	(i) Offsetting transaction for identical contract period (ii) Cancellation of original transaction by negotiation	A position can be unwound at any time	Can be arranged by negotiation with original counterparty

Short-term hedging techniques (*cont.*)			
	Forward-rate agreements	Financial futures	Interest-rate guarantees (options)
Margin requirements	None	Initial and variation margin	None
Credit lines	Limit required	None	No limit if customer buys guarantee
Availability	Good	Good	Good
Charges	None	Small commission payment to broker	Premium (see Price quotations above)
Administration	Only at settlement	Daily marked to market with margin payments	Payment of premium and at settlement

Collars

The third element of the trinity, the interest-rate collar, might help if the question of cost is proving a stumbling block, since such a contract can reduce or perhaps eliminate the up-front charge.

The collar is a combination of a cap and a floor and in effect locks interest rates into a specified range. For instance, if a company is borrowing $20 million on a floating-rate basis and believes interest rates are going to rise, it can, instead of entering into a straightforward cap deal, buy an interest-rate collar which will establish both floor and cap. If interest rates at the time of the agreement are 10 per cent, it would set the cap at 12 per cent and the floor at 8 per cent.

The premium it pays to the bank is smaller than if it were to buy just a cap because, by setting a floor on the interest rate, it would forgo any gain if the rate fell below the agreed level, in this instance 8 per cent. If the rate fell below that level to, say, 6 per cent, the company would have to compensate the bank for the value of the difference between the floor rate and the lower interest-rate level. It would of course still benefit from a rise in interest rates above the agreed level in the same way that it would from a cap.

Long-term hedging techniques			
	Forward forwards	Interest-rate swaps	Caps, collars and floors
Currencies	Most major currencies	All major currencies, including US$, £, DM, SFr, yen, C$ and A$	Principal market in US$. Others including £, DM, SFr and yen available on a more restricted basis
Amounts	No preset figures but minimum around US$1m (or eq.)	Min.: approx. US$5m (or eq.)	Min.: approx. US$5m (or eq.)
Price quotations	Spreads wider than FRAs or financial futures	Good two-way prices available from banks	Normally a single price quoted for transaction. (A two-way price would be fairly wide.)
Flexibility	Amounts and periods tailored to customer needs	Amounts and periods tailored to customer needs	Amounts and periods tailored to customer needs. (Maximum period shorter than for interest-rate swap.)
Premium	No	No	Yes, payable upfront
Impact of favourable changes in interest rates	Agreement fixed for term of deal	Agreement fixed for term of deal	Ability to benefit from favourable interest-rate movements
Impact of adverse changes in interest rates	Agreement fixed for term of deal	Agreement fixed for term of deal	Worst rate fixed by levels of cap, collar or floor as appropriate

Long-term hedging techniques (*cont.*)			
	Forward forwards	Interest-rate swaps	Caps, collars and floors
Margin requirements	Nil	Nil	Nil
Credit lines	Limit required for loans	Limit needed	No limit if company buys cap or floor. Limit needed for collar and if company wishes to write cap or floor.
Reversal of transaction	More difficult than FRAs or financial futures. Can be arranged by negotiation with original counterparty.	Can be arranged	Cap, collar or floor can be sold back to counterparty based on current valuation.
Availability	Limited	Good	Good

An investor, as well as a borrower, can use this device to reduce the cost of a contract. An investor would buy a floor and sell a cap, but in doing so would face a similar penalty to that of the borrower seeking to protect itself. If interest rates rose above the cap level the company would forego a potential gain, just as the borrower in effect loses out if interest rates fall below the level the company has agreed.

Interest-rate swaps are another technique used to manage risks (see pp. 89–90).

8. Currency exposure management

In the past, UK exporters would almost always have asked to be paid in sterling, and many still do. But as sterling has declined in importance, importers have become less willing to pay in it. These days, exporters should always consider accepting a foreign currency: if importers are allowed to pay in their own currency, they are absolved of exchange risk – a loss caused by an adverse currency movement between the signature of the contract and the payment date. In some cases, importers will prefer to pay in a third currency in which they have income (the oil states like to pay in US dollars, for example). Either way, the exporter will receive money in a foreign currency.

You can, of course, exchange foreign currency into sterling at the prevailing or 'spot' rate when you receive it. Some companies will speculate on currency movements when they sign contracts, and may decide that the odds on the currency appreciating against sterling are sufficiently good that they do not need to protect themselves. But there are sufficient stories of companies catching cold in this way that most sellers choose to hedge – that is, to lock themselves into a certain rate after signing the contract so that they know exactly how much sterling they will receive.

Hedging

Foreign currency account

Before looking at the most common hedging device, forward exchange contracts, we should consider a simpler mechanism, the currency account. This is simply a bank account opened in Deutschemarks, dollars, or whatever. It can be opened at any major bank branch, and often overseas branches of the UK banks.

Two sorts of exporter should consider these accounts. First, those who have a regular two-way flow of transactions in a different currency. Most currency fluctuations will simply be cancelled out, and a far smaller amount has to be transferred back into sterling. Second, those who have a large number of receipts or payments in a currency.

They can be bulked up and exchanged in one go, saving on administrative costs and benefiting from better rates on large deals.

When there is a gap between receipts and payments, you may be able to arrange an overdraft to cover it.

Forward exchange contracts

There is a well-established mechanism for taking the risk out of foreign currency transactions: the forward exchange market. Using this, you can make a binding agreement with your bank – a forward exchange contract – to switch one currency for another at a specific date (or perhaps within a range of dates) and at a particular rate. It does not matter what the spot rate does between the signature of the contract and payment; you know exactly how much you will receive in sterling. A recent example of the importance of this mechanism was a major car producer's decision to take out forward exchange contracts for up to two years ahead; this meant that it was able to exchange its important dollar receipts at less than $1.60 to the pound when the spot rate was approaching $2.00.

Interest rates

Whether the forward rate is higher than the spot rate or not depends largely on the interest-rate difference between the two currencies. In theory, a low interest rate currency will appreciate against a high interest rate currency. In the short term, this theory rarely holds true

---

Example

An exporter to West Germany makes a sale for DM100,000; the exporter will be paid in three months' time. The bank shows him these figures:

	Bank sells	Bank buys
Spot rates	DM3.1820	DM3.1850
3 months	0.0615 premium	0.0600 premium
Forward rate	3.1205	3.1250

The exporter enters a forward contract to sell the DM100,000 to the bank in three months' time. The premium is deducted; the forward rate is more favourable than the spot.

At this rate, the exporter will receive £32,000 against the £31,397 he would get at the current spot rate. This may seem like a straight advantage but it merely reflects the difference in interest income that he is forgoing over three months. It is, however, clear that the exporter can make extra profit from using a forward contract, or can reduce his price in Deutschemark terms.

(which is why some firms attempt to beat it by not covering forward), but it does provide a useful and simple way of calculating rates. Usually, if the interest rate of the currency is lower than sterling, then it will be at a premium to the spot rate; if higher, it will be at a discount.

Currency baskets and the ecu

A way of reducing exchange risk without taking out a forward contract is to use a currency basket or cocktail. Particularly relevant for EC trade is the ecu. The ecu is simply a weighted average of the currencies of the EC and, as such, is likely to fluctuate less than any of them. The ecu was originally created to settle transactions between governments, but has become quite popular in trade finance and other banking transactions because of its stability. Major banks should be able to offer a range of services, including accounts and spot and forward exchange quotations, in ecus. An additional advantage of the ecu in trade with the EC is that there is a pan-European clearing system, which means it can be treated in exactly the same way as sterling.

Currency options

These are comparatively new financial instruments that can provide a more flexible form of exchange risk cover. The options market gives the exporter the right, but not the obligation, to buy or sell foreign currency at a certain rate on or before a particular date. The currency option has parallels with insurance. It brings a far greater degree of risk to the person issuing it (the writer) than an ordinary foreign exchange deal, so the writer is paid a premium to cover that risk. As an option is an asset, it will have some value if it is unused, provided that a reasonable time remains before it matures.

Options have three main uses in trade. First, they allow the exporter to take advantage of a favourable movement in the spot rate, while sticking to the option if that gives a better rate when payment is made. This is still a gamble. The profit on the movement will have to be more than the cost of the premium, otherwise it would have been better to use the forward market.

Tender-to-contract cover

The second use is where the selling company is not sure whether it is going to win the business. Typically, a contractor making a bid, and quoting in a foreign currency, will want to cover its exchange risk from the moment of tendering, but cannot be certain enough to take out forward cover until it wins the contract. Options have become increasingly important for providing tender-to-contract cover.

The third use is where a company is uncertain how much currency it is going to need. A holiday company, for example, could cover 80 per cent of its exposure on the forward market – because it knows it will definitely need that much – but use options to protect itself on the balance.

The commonest way for companies to buy options contracts is over-the-counter from banks, which tailor them in amounts and maturities to suit a customer's specific requirements. Options can also be bought on exchanges such as LIFFE, where they are standardised contracts which come in set amounts and for set periods. Generally speaking, exchange-traded financial instruments are less flexible than those available over-the-counter from banks, which is why companies tend to favour over-the-counter options.

Banks will write options for most sizes of companies, from major corporates down to relatively small firms. The minimum contract size is around £50,000. The two main questions an options writer will ask itself are: Is the company in a position to pay the premium for the option and, If the option is exercised, is the company in a position to provide the necessary counter-currency?

Futures

Exchanges also offer currency futures contracts, which can be used as hedging tools. Such a contract is an agreement to buy or sell a set amount of currency at a set date at a set price. Futures differ from options in that they must be exercised at the set date and there is no over-the-counter market.

9. Currency and interest-rate swaps

The currency and interest-rate swap markets were among the first of the new developments in international finance during the 1970s, and have thrived to become the most successful innovations of that decade. It is natural that Company A with an exposure in an inconvenient currency should seek out Company B whose exposure is in a currency more attractive to A and offer to 'swap' the currencies. Interest-rate risks work on the same principle.

From such a simple proposition two vast markets have grown. Currency swaps outstanding were worth around $90 billion in January 1987 and interest-rate swaps no less than $350 billion. The size of the markets clearly indicates the value to businesses of these excellent mechanisms for managing risk.

The currency swap market was the first to develop and came as a natural response to the new uncertainties over the US dollar in the late 1960s and early 1970s. A UK company which borrowed dollars for future repayment faced an obvious problem at that time: What would be the exchange rate on the dollar at the end of the term and did this risk fit the company's trading profile?

Currency swaps

The swap solution was for the UK company and its US creditor (effectively a bank) to agree to buy specific amounts of each other's currency from each other at the spot price and then sell the same amounts back at the end of the term; the trick was that the same exchange rate was used on both transactions, and that the two parties made regular payments to each other at an agreed rate over the term of the deal.

In effect, the UK group which owed dollars would make the equivalent interest payment in sterling and repay the loan in sterling at the end of the term. Meanwhile, the US bank would be paying interest on the dollar loan to the UK company and at the end of the term would repay the dollar loan principal sum.

For the UK group, the advantage is that a dollar liability has been converted into a sterling liability which is more convenient to the UK company's trading profile. The same principles can be applied to any acceptable currency liability.

International loans, like the domestic variety, are arranged on either

Interest-rate swaps

fixed or variable rates, as well as at high or low levels of interest. Floating rates are usually linked to LIBOR. There have always been good accounting reasons for borrowers to prefer a fixed-rate liability to a floating-rate one. Interest-rate swaps were introduced to facilitate the switch from one to the other; but they are also used for many other more sophisticated purposes.

Interest-rate swaps differ from currency swaps in that only the interest liability is swapped. No funds are lent or borrowed: this is important because it enables these deals to be regarded as off-balance-sheet transactions. The underlying loan is unaffected by the swap agreement, which concerns only interest payments. The interest payments between the two parties are normally 'netted out' so that the minimum of cash transfer is required. This is another significant point of difference from currency swaps, where payments, being due in different currencies, have to be made in full. Thus, a company unhappy with the debt interest liabilities set at six-month LIBOR plus 1 per cent will arrange a swap under which a bank will pay its six-month LIBOR for the agreed term; in return, the company pays the bank an agreed fixed rate over the term of the agreement.

On this fairly simple basis, complicated interest-rate swaps can be constructed. Swaps can include a 'delayed' or 'stepped' start, whereby the swap begins part of the way through the loan term. Interest payments can be level throughout or varied to suit the customer's requirements.

The advantage of swap agreements is that they allow alterations to be made in currency or interest-rate flows without disturbing the underlying assets and liabilities. Customers with heavy trade liabilities in France will prefer to receive a substantial portion of their overseas revenue in French francs; they will do this by swapping their Swiss franc inflows. Customers with an active borrowing profile may prefer to make interest payments which follow interest trends; they will swap fixed-rate for variable-rate payments. Customers cannot be certain of obtaining access to the relevant term loan markets at any given moment. Swap arrangements enable them to overcome such obstacles and are often relatively cheap compared with conventional access to capital markets. They are simple to arrange and require the minimum of documentation.

This being an imperfect world, swaps are not without complications, particularly in their tax and accounting treatment. However, the benefits of swaps far outweigh the potential problems and erratic debt markets mean that swaps are here to stay. That said, the impetus given to liberalisation of the capital markets by the run up to 1992 will reduce some of the motivation for using swaps.

10. Limited recourse finance

Thus far we have covered short-term trade-related finance, and alternative methods of short-term, medium-term and long-term borrowing. We have also looked at how to manage interest-rate and foreign exchange risk. There are other approaches and sources of finance which do not fall neatly into the above categories. They are limited recourse finance, leasing (Chapter 11), franchising (Chapter 12) and EC loans and grants (Chapter 13).

Large projects often require specialist financing, arranged by either the project sponsor or by the contractor in support of a bid. The wide variety of options might include capital issues, export credits, bilateral and multilateral aid and limited recourse finance.

Limited recourse finance, also known as project finance, has been available for several years, but the concept is not always fully understood. Broadly speaking, it can be defined as 'finance for a project wholly or partly on the credit of the project itself, with the revenue from the completed project being the sole or primary source of repayment'.

Numerous sectors lend themselves to this form of finance. In the EC, North Sea oil- and gas-fields were the first recipients of project finance in the 1970s. Today, the emphasis has changed away from resource projects. Sectors most suited to limited recourse finance include infrastructure (toll roads, bridges and tunnels), power generation, industrial processing and leisure (such as theme parks and satellite television). Over the past few years, especially in the UK and now in Europe as a whole, there has been a surge in these kinds of projects. Private sector companies have been expanding into areas previously the sole preserve of governments. Projects financed, or to be financed, in such a way by UK banks include the Broadgate office development in London, the £5 billion Eurotunnel and the Dartford River Crossing.

The public sector Open public procurement in the EC, which should occur with the creation of the single market, will make it easier for UK firms to tender for large projects in other member states. Some of these projects will lend themselves to limited recourse finance; to do so, they must be definable projects with assessable income streams that are adequate to serve the debt required.

The borrower's objectives

With limited recourse finance, the borrowing companies limit their obligations to the lenders by restricting the lenders' interest and repayment rights to the assets and revenues of the project. In other words, the lenders have 'limited recourse' to the companies behind the project, which effectively means that the lenders share some of the risk; but the lenders have full recourse to the single purpose company and the project. Another advantage of this form of finance for the borrowing companies is that it may minimise the guarantees and contingent liabilities in its consolidated accounts.

Generally, the borrowing companies will have one or more of the following objectives:

- To transfer some of the project risk to the lenders

- To match repayments to the project revenues

- To maximise the amount which can be raised against project assets

- To reduce the impact of financing on its balance sheet, thereby maintaining flexibility for further borrowing and making it easier to ensure compliance with any existing loan agreements

- To isolate the security and to avoid cross-default provisions

The lenders' consideration of risks

In not having full recourse to the individual balance sheets of the sponsors, lenders have to assess risk based on the fact that they can only be repaid from the project revenues. There are, broadly speaking, technical, economic and political risks.

Technical Given the size, complexity and variety of projects, lenders use independent consultants to examine technical risks. Lenders will want to be satisfied that the project sponsor is capable of arranging a project that is technically viable within certain costs, that is in accordance with any guidelines and anticipated contractual terms, that will pass completion tests and that will function adequately throughout its expected operational life.

Economic Independent consultants will be used to assess economic risks. The lenders will want to be sure that the project will generate sufficient income to service the limited recourse debt. For instance, infrastructure projects, such as a motorway or tunnel, can be repaid from charges levied for their use, and lenders will want to be satisfied that the operators will charge economic tariffs. In the case of projects which derive their income from depleting assets, such as oil or gas, lenders will not only be taking the risk that the product will not be sold at an economic price, but that not enough of the product will be recoverable.

Political Political risks include changes in taxation, which could affect a project's viability. Lenders may therefore structure a limited recourse finance package on a pre-tax basis, leaving the tax risk with the borrower. There are also non-fiscal risks such as expropriation without compensation, revoking of licences, controls on production and foreign exchange controls.

Loan amount

The amount lent depends on the forecast revenues of a project. These revenues are discounted over the proposed life at the lenders' perceived average interest rate for that period, thus determining the net present value. The ratio of the net present value to the amount of the

Cover ratio loan outstanding at any time is the cover ratio. The level of cover ratio will reflect the lenders' perception of the risks involved. A depleting asset project will usually need a higher ratio in order to provide adequate cover for the perceived risks, while an infrastructure project, which has a greater degree of certainty about the revenues it will generate, will usually have a lower ratio.

Repayment

Lenders will require that minimum repayments are made over the life of the loan, with a provision that if the repayments fall behind, they may be increased up to 100 per cent of the project's cash flow. The project should have a significant life-span remaining after the loan has matured.

The role of the banks

Over the years major international banks have become more willing to assume limited recourse risks as they have grown more familiar with them. In the first substantial North Sea financing, for BP's Forties Field, banks would assume only the reservoir risk – that is, the risk of the forecast amounts of oil not being there, but not the risk of technical or economic problems arising. Nowadays, many lenders assume these technical and economic risks. Large project financing is frequently managed by a lead bank which will syndicate the loan amongst other banks.

The key point for contractors to remember is to involve the banks from the outset. The banks must be allowed to assess the eligibility and viability of a project. There is no point in signing contracts without first being sure of getting the necessary finance.

11. Leasing

1992 and the elimination of barriers between EC member states could have a dramatic impact on leasing, which has become more important as a financial instrument in recent years. Leasing is no longer confined to one country, but extends across frontiers and this particularly applies to what is known as big ticket leasing, involving purchases of ships, tankers, aircraft, oil refineries and large plant and machinery.

Yet the problem is that leasing is not the same product in all countries. The EC does not have a common definition of leasing, let alone a common tax treatment for leasing. In the UK a financial lease is one where the lessor owns the assets and recovers over the lease period the costs of the assets, the finance charges and the profit. At the end of the period the asset is sold to a third party.

The UK saw a great boom in leasing in the 1970s and the early 1980s, which particularly benefited banks and financial institutions. Their profits were subject to corporation tax at 52 per cent, yet they did not have many assets that qualified for capital allowances, nor did they have much stock that qualified for the reliefs that were introduced to deal with the high inflation raging in the mid-1970s. On the other hand, there were many industrial and commercial companies which were not able to make use of their capital allowances because they did not generate sufficient profits. So leasing in the UK developed as a means by which banks and financial institutions transmitted in reduced rentals the benefits of capital allowances to users who would otherwise have been unable to enjoy them.

UK tax changes
Some of the glitter has gone as a result of recent tax changes, the reduction of corporation tax and the abolition of 100 per cent first-year allowances which had played a part in the growth of the UK equipment-leasing industry. Even so, leasing remains important and is still very much a 'tax priced' product in this country. In other words, in the UK leasing arrangements reflect the benefit of tax allowances.

This is not so, however, in France and West Germany, for example, which along with the UK make up the big three in EC leasing. In these countries leasing prevails as a service and it is very different. In France there is something called *crédit-bail*, which is equivalent to the UK's hire purchase except that the financier gets the benefit of capital allowances. In West Germany, leasing is closer to France than the UK as long as the lease agreement falls between 40 per cent and 90 per cent of asset life. If it continues longer than that, then the lessee rather than the lessor can claim tax allowances. The lessee's option price of purchase is normally equal to the tax-written-down value.

Capital allowances

There is also wide disparity in the way the capital allowances work. UK allowances work on 25 per cent reducing-balance method and the asset is written off in about sixteen years. In France and West Germany the assets can be written off within a five- to ten-year period, which means the benefit is obtained earlier.

Tax treatment of overseas leases

The most interesting debate about leasing and 1992 concerns what will happen in the tax treatment of overseas leases. This has great significance for UK business. At present, if a UK company has an overseas lease, then the lease is treated differently from a UK lease. The lessor, on an overseas lease, can claim allowances of only 10 per cent on a reducing-balance method, hedged by restrictions, over thirteen years. This means the tax allowance benefit passed on the lessee is smaller, and, therefore, the leasing arrangement is more expensive. So once the barriers come down in 1992 and the EC is one unit as far as trade is concerned, should not the UK company be allowed to apply the UK leasing arrangements for overseas deals? This subject is being much debated by the Equipment Leasing Association and the answer could prove crucial.

If the differences between a domestic lease and an overseas lease disappeared, so would some of the absurdities. If a lessor writes a lease for the French subsidiary of a UK company, then it is an overseas lease. If it is done for a French branch of a UK company, then it is a domestic lease attracting the lower domestic leasing rates. Such quirks will have to be resolved by 1992.

Restricting overseas leases to the 10 per cent allowance means that at the moment cross-border 'big ticket' leases are priced out of the market. Suppose Air France wanted to buy something from British Aerospace. This, in theory, could be a 'big ticket' leasing arrangement. But because of the 10 per cent allowance system, such a big ticket leasing would not be competitive with other forms of finance that Air France could arrange. A Japanese leveraged lease would be cheaper. It would be cheaper still for a French leasing company to acquire and lease the aircraft to Air France. This means that present UK tax laws deprive the UK financial community of the chance of financing a deal that is in the interests of a major UK exporter. Changes in UK tax legislation will clearly be needed if the EC is to be treated as a domestic market and some of these anomalies removed.

In addition to this there is a need for greater harmonisation of the leasing rules and customs in the EC. This will not be easy, since member states have great national pride in their leasing arrangements and in recent times international meetings held to sort out these problems have produced a great deal of emotional debate but few solutions.

Leveraged leasing

One consequence of 1992 may be that the UK gets leveraged leasing as exists in other countries, including France. This form of leasing is particularly popular in the USA and involves the lessor having any-thing between 20 and 25 per cent as equity, with the rest borrowed from a third party, possibly a bank. It can have balance-sheet advantages for the lessor, since certain things can go off-balance-sheet. Also the return required by the financing bank is lower than that required by the lessor. This is non-recourse lending by the banks and they look to the rental stream to get their repayments.

If the trade and financial barriers really come down by 1992, it will mean a bigger leasing market for the UK financial institutions and it could make the domestic leasing market in certain member states a great deal more competitive. The UK is by no means ahead of the field. In 1986 the UK equipment leasing market was worth £5.2 billion as against Fr 31 billion (£3.1 billion) for the French market and DM23 billion (£7.6 billion) for the dominant West German market. There is clearly a lot to play for and if greater competition does indeed result, the attractiveness of leasing for large-scale capital investment in the UK and the EC should be enhanced still further.

12.   Franchising

Expansion is always difficult and often dangerous, particularly for small companies in the retail market offering goods and services to the public. When planning to increase the number of outlets, one of the first considerations, along with finance and logistics, is how to retain a reputation for a crisp and customer-oriented service. A branch operation which tarnishes that image could eventually drag down the whole business. The owner has to ensure that throughout the branch network staff remain motivated and standards are up to scratch. Yet the owner cannot be everywhere at once.

Franchising can often be the solution. It is a relatively new concept in the UK, though well established in the USA. While definitions of franchising are broadly the same the world over, in the UK and other member states business-format franchising dominates, while in the USA a great many other types of business, operating under what we would call simple licences, are included.

The business that wishes to franchise is essentially allowing others to use its unique product or service and system, and the business name and image, to repeat its success in new markets, in return for a fee and a percentage of the new business generated.

In its early days in the UK franchising had a poor image. Unproven ideas were sold by fast-talking salesmen to unsophisticated would-be entrepreneurs and there were several unhappy outcomes. However, today, thanks to the British Franchise Association (BFA), the industry operates mostly along established guidelines and has become a relatively safe path not only for the franchisor – the owner of the business – but equally for the franchisee – the independent 'subsidiary' of the original company.

Terms   The agreement between franchisor and franchisee is complex but essentially it defines the term of the contract, the rights of renewal, the ownership of the franchisee site and the obligations that each has to the other. The franchisor will agree to train the franchisee in its system and to permit the franchisee to operate an exact copy of the business within a specific geographical area. The agreement will allow the franchisor to retain control over the manner in which the business is carried out and spell out the conditions under which the contract can

Pilot scheme

be cancelled or the franchise withdrawn. It will also lay out the terms of the financial agreement – the size and the nature of the initial fee and the ongoing service fees, as well as any agreement concerning the supply of materials needed to carry on the business. The franchisee will be buying a proven concept, and it is essential that the concept is just that. The franchisor must have had a pilot scheme, usually its own business, up and running long enough to demonstrate without any doubt that its unique concept and method of running the operation can succeed and can produce a reward sufficient to attract franchisees. Usually franchisees are expected to demonstrate their commitment to their enterprise by contributing a third to a half of start-up costs themselves. The major clearing banks will often contribute the rest in the form of a loan to the franchisee, usually secured on the franchisee's assets.

Franchising can provide the answer to the problems of expansion that have been perplexing the successful company. By creating a copy of its own business it can generate expansion. By licensing someone else to operate this copy as an independent business it is giving the franchisee the motivation to inject that element of personal sacrifice that can spell the difference between an average service and one that sparkles and attracts customers. And because the franchisee provides, with the help of the banks, the start-up finance, there is less strain on the resources of the franchisor.

British Franchise Association

The essential element in the success of any company expansion via the franchise route is the BFA, an organisation that represents virtually all the major franchisors in the country. It exercises, though it sounds contradictory, a powerful voluntary control over the ethics and standards of the franchise industry. It was set up in 1977 to act on behalf of franchisors but, particularly of late, it has become active on behalf of the franchisees, setting up, amongst other things, an arbitration scheme with the Institute of Arbitrators for the settlement of franchisor–franchisee disputes. The BFA is, therefore, the first port of call for both sides when they make their initial moves along the franchise route. The BFA is an invaluable source of information on all aspects of franchising and no sensible franchisor or franchisee ought to consider making plans or decisions without having consulted the BFA.

Most of the clearing banks are heavily involved in aiding the franchising industry and have set up franchise departments. Franchise consultants have begun to appear. They can be a useful follow-up to discussions with the BFA and the banks.

It should be noted briefly that while franchising can permit the single outlet company to grow easily into one of multiple outlets, it can also be used effectively for businesses with several company-owned outlets.

**Franchisors'
options**

1992 is likely to have an effect on the growth of franchising in the EC. UK franchisors are already invading the EC market and it is likely that the arrival of the single market will serve to speed up the invasion.

There are a number of paths into the EC available to franchisors. They can set up their own chain of franchisees in just the same way as they would in the UK. They can also expand by making acquisitions and then converting the units into franchisee outlets. A third option is to mount a joint venture with another company. However, probably the most practical in funding terms as well as in sheer logistics is for the franchisor to sell a regional or national licence to someone in the country of expansion, and let them take the operation forward for the franchisor. The licensee has the advantage of business and banking contacts in their own country. They might choose to expand the business through company-owned units, or through franchising, or a mixture of both, depending on what is likely to work best in the circumstances. The licensee would pay the franchisor a fee on signing the agreement which would specify some performance target (a fixed number of outlets per year, for example). There can be an additional fee on the opening of each unit and/or a percentage on gross network sales.

Anyone in the UK considering franchising in Europe would be well advised to call on the franchise departments of the various major clearing banks at an early stage. Some have extensive contacts in the EC already set up, some are stronger in some countries than others. As always in business, the secret of success is to shop around and select the bank that seems to offer the best facilities, allied to experience, in that particular field.

Each member state has its own franchise association, and all are affiliated to the European Franchise Federation in Brussels. Your bankers can put you in touch either with the local association direct, or with the Federation. There is always the longshot that your bank will also be able to help you find a licensee from among its customers in the EC, but it is more than likely you will have to find your EC partner yourself. UK banks with a retail operation should be able to help you in the financing of your expansion. Even when they have only a wholesale operation and deal only with major businesses, you may still find, if you have chosen your bank wisely, that they can help with the introduction to a franchise-wise indigenous bank. Remember, by the way, that if you are strong enough, you could take a stake in the European company yourself.

Franchising is steadily growing in importance in the business community. Properly handled it can allow a business to expand without any of the traditional drawbacks associated with a larger company and its dealings with the individual customer. But it is still a system that, relatively speaking, is in its infancy and it is essential to proceed not only with caution, but also in concert with those who know most about the industry – the various franchise associations and the clearing banks.

13. Sources of EC finance

Direct finance

European Community funds can be a major source of finance for companies, both directly and indirectly. The direct method of receiving finance is where the EC makes loans and grants direct to companies in the various member states. Most UK firms which apply for direct finance use it for business expansion at home. But there is nothing to stop them applying for finance to establish operations or win business in other member states. They would be subject to just the same criteria as domestic applicants in the other countries.

Indirect finance

The indirect method of finance is where the EC makes loans and grants to central governments, local authorities, and other public bodies for large projects; these bodies then award contracts to businesses from their own or other member states, ranging from large contractors to small enterprises. Most EC finance is of the indirect kind; and for UK companies hoping to win contracts in the EC, one of the keys to success is to get information ahead of competitors about specific projects being funded.

With all funding, preference is given to recipients in industries and regions suffering from economic problems, with an emphasis on job creation. Cross-frontier collaboration is also encouraged, as are projects which will help the EC compete in the global arena.

How the EC obtains money

The EC obtains money in two ways. The first is from its own resources, which are made up of a proportion of all the states' VAT revenues, customs duties, agricultural levies and additional contributions from each state based on their GNP. The second method is by issuing bonds on the international capital markets.

Where does the finance go? Opportunities for UK businesses

The Community budget has to be set each year, and this is often the cause of much disagreement. Roughly speaking, 68 per cent is spent on agriculture; 16 per cent on regional, social and farm modernisation; 5 per cent on administration; 4 per cent on rebates to the

UK, Spain and Portugal; 3 per cent on overseas development; 2 per cent on industrial and research policies; and 2 per cent on other matters.

Allocation of funds

The money is allocated by a number of bodies. The main ones are the three Structural Funds: the European Social Fund, the European Regional Development Fund and the European Agricultural Guidance and Guarantee Fund. The European Coal and Steel Community (ECSC) and European Investment Bank (EIB) are also important sources of finance. UK companies seeking to benefit from these funds in the UK and other member states can contact these bodies direct (see Appendix 3 for contact addresses), but it would be advisable in the first instance for them to contact the Department of Trade and Industry (DTI), which has a central department dealing with EC finance. Other useful contact points are the leading UK banks and the commercial officers of UK embassies.

Structural Funds

The European Council decided in 1988 to increase the Structural Funds' annual budget from £5 billion a year to £10 billion a year by 1993. The main part of the extra money will go to Portugal, Greece, the Republic of Ireland, Italy and Spain. Added to that will be about £7 billion to help finance the Barcelona Olympics and Expo '92 in Seville. The DTI believes this increase should 'provide valuable opportunities' for UK businesses to win contracts abroad, both in preliminary work (such as advising authorities on preparing projects to submit to the Commission for approval), and in project management and implementation. Typical projects will be for roads, railways, water works, factory equipment and the development of tourism.

The Commission's desire to bring about open public procurement in the Community should make it easier for UK firms to tender for contracts. In order to win such contracts it may be necessary to go into joint ventures with local companies in the countries concerned. UK

UK share

companies have not done particularly well in winning EC-funded contracts. To date, French firms have won 35 per cent of projects funded by Structural Funds, West German firms 20 per cent and UK firms 5 per cent. The reasons for this may be that UK contractors already have enough work at home and are not especially hungry for more, and also that they have been slower than their competitors to get advance information of the funded projects. Nevertheless, Costain, Laing and Trafalgar House have all been successful in winning Community projects.

Greece

Greece, because of the large amount of EC structural funding it will receive between now and 1993, provides evidence of the sorts of opportunities that UK companies might exploit with the help of EC finance. According to a DTI report on Greece, UK exporters should focus on selling to those general areas which are likely to benefit from EC structural funding, since those sectors will have more money available for purchases. The massive funding for Greece's infrastructure development, for example, should mean that the market for civil engineering and construction equipment will be buoyant. 'Major areas of direct opportunities for goods or services, particularly specialist consultancies,' says the DTI's report *European Structural Funds in Greece*, 'would include infrastructure, tourism development, crop diversification, food processing and marketing, training, fish farming, systems management and the development of communications and public administration.' EC-funded projects in Greece are open to bidders from all states, but it is important to have a local agency or partnership agreement to stand a good chance. It is crucial in some cases, says the DTI report: 'An effective presence in Greece will be the *only* way of obtaining information about small-scale state procurements or procurements by the private sector using EC-financed investment incentives.'

The European Social Fund (ESF)

Training

This is primarily a fund for improving job opportunities for workers through training and re-training. Grants are directed at regions or groups of workers most in need. Generally speaking, at least 75 per cent of resources are allocated to people under twenty-five.

The ESF will usually reimburse 50 per cent of the cost of re-training schemes financed by public authorities, and will part-fund private sector schemes. In 1987, the UK allocation was £436 million, of which £59 million was for Northern Ireland.

In the UK, companies apply through the Department of Employment. UK firms with operations in other member states will apply to the equivalent government departments.

The European Regional Development Fund (ERDF)

The periphery

The ERDF makes grants to help correct disparities of wealth and development within the regions of the Community. The areas with the biggest problems are often on the periphery of the EC: for example, Greece, the Republic of Ireland and Portugal. They also tend to be either under-developed rural areas, or coal, steel, shipbuilding and textiles areas. Most of the ERDF goes to local authorities. But some finance is available directly to companies in badly affected areas

Integrated Mediterranean Programmes for Greece (1986–1992)
(amounts in million ecu)

| IMP | Total expenditure | Community budget | | | | | | | | National public sources | Private sources | EIB(1) |
		*Total	Article 551†	EAGGF	ERDF	ESF	Fishery				
Crete	468.9	240.5	102.5	50.4	86.7	0.9	—			228.4	—	140
Western Greece and the Peloponnese	631.3	361.3	105.8	82.1	153.0	19.0	1.4			179.3	90.7	125
Northern Greece	695.8	406.8	154.5	72.1	150.3	29.9	—			204.9	84.1	120
Central and eastern Greece	550.1	315.6	86.5	58.4	159.8	10.3	0.6			174.0	60.5	117
Attica	407.9	223.1	203.5	2.2	0.6	16.8	—			127.5	57.3	74
Aegean Islands	325.2	193.5	59.5	15.4	114.4	4.1	0.1			103.3	28.4	67
Information technology	134.2	88.8	52.8	—	26.6	9.4	—			45.4	—	12
TOTAL	3,213.4	1,829.6	765.1	280.6	691.4	90.4	2.1			1,062.8	321.0	655

(1) Not included in the financial plan: provisional information which has not yet been made the subject of an EIB Letter of Intent
  * 170m ecu not yet allocated and remaining in reserve for industrial investment
  † Additional funding under Article 551 of the EC Budget

Source: Department of Trade and Industry

Business Improvement Services Scheme

under the Business Improvement Services Scheme. This scheme makes grants, ranging from 55 per cent to 70 per cent, to small and medium-sized companies which need finance for drawing up marketing, management and product development strategies.

UK firms can apply for ERDF grants – or try to win contracts related to ERDF-funded projects – in any member state. The DTI says that as the funds are being greatly increased, 'this will present great commercial opportunities for UK contractors and manufacturing companies especially in the south of Europe'. Companies wanting to apply for ERDF grants can initially get information from UK sources, but ultimately they will have to apply through the DTI-equivalent organisations in the member states concerned.

Taking the UK as an example (the UK gets about 16 per cent of the funds), projects approved for grants in 1988 included the development of Buckland Abbey in Plymouth into a tourist centre (£300,000 grant), the development of a colliery site into workshops in the north of England (£59,000), access roads to two industrial estates in Lancashire (£216,000), industrial estates and small workshops in Yorkshire and Humberside (£1.25 million) and an extension to an industrial estate in Inverness (£462,500).

The European Agricultural Guidance and Guarantee Fund (FEOGA)

This is the principal instrument of the Common Agricultural Policy, and is usually known by its French acronym, FEOGA.

The guarantee section of this fund controls agricultural markets through a complicated system of licences, levies and refunds, and is outside the scope of this text.

The guidance section represents some funding opportunities abroad for UK firms, which could try to win consultancy contracts from public authorities in forestry, horticultural and agricultural engineering, or to supply specialised equipment. But business opportunities under FEOGA are limited, since only 5 per cent of the fund is for the guidance section, and much of that goes to support farming in poorer areas. In the UK, there are some opportunities under the guidance section to win grants for marketing and processing agricultural and fisheries products.

European Coal and Steel Community (ECSC)

The ECSC, which has powers over investment, production and pricing of coal and steel, makes direct loans to qualifying UK businesses. The funds are for modernising the coal and steel industries, and creating new jobs in the areas where these industries are.

Coal and steel

For coal and steel projects, loans of up to 50 per cent of total cost are available at attractive interest rates for fixed capital investment installations that contribute to increasing production, reducing costs and helping marketing. Applications should go direct to the ECSC.

Job-creation

For job-creating projects in industries other than coal and steel, loans at similar rates and with interest rebates can be applied for by private companies or public bodies. Demand has exceeded availability and the Commission has been considering revising the conditions. Applications for loans of more than £10.5 million have to be made to the relevant government department in the country concerned (in the UK, the DTI), not direct to ECSC.

Global loans

For smaller amounts (down to a minimum of £15,001), applications can be made for a 'global loan' through bank branches or development agencies. UK companies wanting a global loan in another member state would have to apply through a bank or development agency in that state. There are certain criteria governing what sorts of businesses can receive global loans, and the banks carry out financial appraisals of each project. The scheme works on the basis that a bank, acting as an intermediary, borrows a large tranche of money from the ECSC and then on-lends in local currency in small 'sub-loans'. These sub-loans may be up to 50 per cent of the project's fixed asset and research and development expenditure. They are repayable over eight years, with a mandatory capital repayment holiday of four years, and are fixed interest. Interest rebates may be given if job creation targets are met.

Loans and grants are also available for companies which intend to improve their workers' housing conditions or provide resettlement allowances and vocational training.

European Investment Bank (EIB)

The EIB is a non-profit-making institution of the Community, but it is not funded out of the Community budget. Its capital is subscribed by the member states, and it gets its operating resources by borrowing on the capital markets. It provides medium- and long-term loans and guarantees to firms, public authorities and financial institutions to help finance the capital costs of certain projects. These projects must promote regional economic development, European integration, European competitiveness or European energy policy.

The EIB makes 'direct loans' in sterling or other currencies direct to borrowers, and not through an intermediary such as a commercial bank. These loans can be used for projects in all sectors of the economy, so long as they meet the basic objectives outlined above. These have included roads, airports, aircraft, ports, telecommunications, water sewerage facilities, energy production, industrial plants and agricultural mining and quarrying projects. If a UK company were to win a contract related to a qualifying project in another member state, it would be able to apply for an EIB loan.

The EIB will finance up to 50 per cent of the fixed assets needed. There is no upper limit, but generally loans will not be less than £1.5 million. The length of the loan can be five to twelve years for industrial projects, and up to twenty years for infrastructure. Interest rates are fixed at the time the contract is signed, and repayment is normally by equal half-yearly payments of capital and interest. Repayment can sometimes be deferred for up to three years. Security is usually required in the form of a guarantee from the government or a bank.

Research and Development Programmes

These include the European Strategic Programme for Research and Development in Information Technologies (ESPRIT), Basic Research in Industrial Technologies for Europe (BRITE) and the European Research Co-ordination Agency (EUREKA). The objective of funding under these programmes is to develop the technological base of EC industry and make it more competitive, especially with the USA and the Far East. Businesses that are successful can get grants of up to 50 per cent of the eligible project.

Environment Programme

Some £17 million is available under this programme for projects such as developing 'clean' technologies, waste recycling and protecting the environment. Grants range from 30 per cent to 75 per cent of project cost.

14. Raising capital funds

Equity

We have concentrated so far on schemes for businesses to raise money externally in the form of debt in order to finance their growth. However, all businesses require an adequate base of internal shareholders' money to support growth, particularly since the uncertainty and the associated risk in developing overseas operations is likely to be greater than in expansion at home.

The prudent level of equity will depend on many factors and the precise circumstances of every business are of course unique. Each, therefore, needs to be considered individually – hence the importance of obtaining good corporate advice when contemplating major developments in your business, whether or not this involves new overseas markets or corporate purchases abroad.

In this chapter, therefore, we look briefly at corporate advisory services and outline considerations of equity for expansion in the EC and opportunities for raising venture capital which may enable business proprietors to off-load some financial risk. The final section on the Eurobond markets is included here because, while in a pure form a Eurobond issue is 'debt' rather than 'equity', it is available only to very large borrowers.

Corporate advisory services

In seeking to meet companies' expansion needs, the banks offer a broad spectrum of services and advice. Smaller companies with a turnover of, say, £1 million upwards and fifty or more people on their payroll can expect a complete service ranging from advice on bank loans, venture capital, the Eurobond markets, partnership links with other companies, acquisitions and stock exchange listings. The aim of any progressive bank is to provide a complete service aimed at covering every possible aspect of a company's financing needs at every stage of its development. On a larger scale, the banks can raise debt for companies on international markets, finance overseas expansion through acquisition or through the development of particular investment projects.

Financing an acquisition

As 1992 and the deadline for the integration of the European Community into a single market draws nearer, so more and more companies of all sizes and at all stages of development will be seeking to expand in the EC by, for example, setting up sales offices, building warehouses and factories, going into joint ventures or acquiring other companies. In the context of acquisitions, banks can put together interim finance either as individual institutions or as part of a syndicate of banks. This can mean that the more permanent funding of an acquisition can be left until the transaction is completed. The bank's role is not, however, merely to finance the acquisition. It may also act as an adviser throughout the transaction, often beginning by finding the appropriate target company for the corporate customer.

Pan-European

The move towards greater European integration will create opportunities for already listed companies to widen and deepen the shareholder base beyond the UK with the expected improvement in the flow of institutional funds within Europe. These additional funds are more likely to flow to those companies which project themselves as pan-European in their style and objectives.

Charges

Normally when acquisitions are being discussed fees are agreed in advance. It is difficult to be specific about charges as they are always subject to negotiation. However, for small acquisitions under £10 million, the fees can be of the order of 2 per cent or more, although the percentage tends to drop significantly as the size of the acquisition increases. For the selling company it is quite normal to add an incentive on to the fee for a high price so that the fee increases considerably after a certain sale price is reached.

Equity considerations

Transnational mergers within the Community have been relatively rare. Increasing integration after 1992 seems destined to make such transnational mergers increasingly common. Already a trend towards the cross-ownership of EC companies, which collaborate by swapping strategic shareholdings in each other, is beginning to gain momentum as the date for integration approaches. Collaborative efforts in such areas as defence, civil aviation, telecommunications, electronics and, more recently, in broadcasting and the media, are leading to joint bids and mutual share-swapping arrangements.

Liquidity

As the use of equity to forge links across the EC increases, there is likely to be more liquidity available from EC financial institutions for those companies seeking to become pan-European. Much of this increased supply of liquidity for investment in the equity of companies is likely to be channelled to London, which remains the Community's pre-eminent financial centre. Institutional funds for equity investment already move freely across EC borders, but the investment philosophy of institutions is likely to become more pan-European in outlook. This creates opportunities for companies seeking further equity finance for expansion in the EC.

In the UK the cult of the equity is already well established among the financial institutions. Broadly speaking, some 40 per cent of all their funds are invested in ordinary shares. In other member states, the institutionally backed equity market is much less well developed. In West Germany, for example, only about 5 per cent of institutional funds are in ordinary shares. In France, Spain and Italy equity (or the equity market) is again not as well developed as it is in the UK.

The single market will inevitably bring increased competition in financial services as more institutions in the Community begin to offer the range of services similar to those already on offer from UK institutions and begin to adopt a more positive attitude to the provision of equity finance.

Equity supply

In the UK there appears to be no danger of the supply of new equity running out. Latest estimates suggest that, despite the issue of an estimated £14 billion of new equity on to the market during 1988, an almost equivalent sum was withdrawn from the stock market through cash takeover bids. This left UK institutions' steady appetite for equities unimpaired. Had the Government not raised some £6 billion during the year from privatisations, the supply of equity to the market would have shrunk by almost that amount. UK institutional cash flows are such that on average between £23 billion and £26 billion becomes available for investment each year. The Government, in the process of reducing the National Debt, has cut the supply of government stock available for absorbing the institutional cash flows. So, even though the UK equity market has lately put up a distinctly uninspiring performance, institutions here are expected to invest something like £9 billion in the market in 1988 and possibly £11 billion in 1989.

EC institutions are taking note of the investment approach of UK insurance and other financial institutions. Two significant UK insurance groups, Equity and Law and Cornhill Insurance have already been acquired by EC companies and their approach to equity investment may well influence the attitude of their parent companies – the French Compagnie du Midi in Equity and Law's case, and Allianz of West Germany in Cornhill's case.

West Germany

In West Germany, where the population is ageing, the market for insurance and pension products is ripe for the sort of financial packages, available from leading UK insurance companies, which use long-term investment in equities to provide backing for steady growth in income capital. In the 1970s the Investors Overseas Services débâcle deterred investment in equities in West Germany for ten years and the crash of 1987 did nothing to encourage its revival. However, the German insurance industry is gradually placing increasing emphasis on equity investment. While German insurance companies have only 2.5 per cent of their total assets in equities, the proportion of new money going into equities has now increased to 10 per cent and may rise rapidly over the next few years. UK companies may be able to provide the German insurance and pensions market with the increased equity opportunity it needs. UK industry needs to acquire German companies to expand in this important market and to acquire German industrial know-how. Many major UK companies have already made such acquisitions. Medium-sized and smaller groups should now be considering the opportunities available.

France

In France the stock-market has been rejuvenated during the past five years. New settlement systems, the development of a futures market and the growth of an indigenous unit trust movement have created a more attractive environment for equity investment. At the same time, industry, much of which remains under state control, is undergoing considerable re-structuring, initially through privatisation but more recently through the more selective sale of shares in subsidiaries. Here, too, liquidity is building up among local financial institutions. This trend, coupled with the re-structuring of industry, creates opportunities for UK business to expand in France. In the private sector, local companies are certainly not invulnerable to foreign takeover and some opportunities have already been seized by UK companies (the recent links forged by Guinness with Moët Hennessy, for example).

Italy

The Italian government has recently altered the rules to allow local institutions greater freedom to invest overseas. This is potentially a significant new source of liquidity which has not been available outside Italy since the mid-1970s. Italian industry remains dominated by the major business dynasties of Agnelli, De Benedetti and Gardini, while the two state-sponsored enterprises ENI and IRI are also a major influence on ownership in the private sector. The most likely way for UK companies to expand through acquisition in the Italian market is through joint-venture agreements rather than wholesale acquisitions.

Portugal and Spain

The Portuguese and Spanish markets are full of potential. Portugal has an underdeveloped equities market but the Portuguese have a high savings ratio and labour costs are low relative to the rest of the EC. Europe, faced with intensified competition from the Far East in such products as consumer durables, cars and textiles, is turning increasingly to Portugal to provide solutions to manufacturing problems.

Portugal is quite simply the cheapest production base in the Community and any UK company wishing to start a greenfield project should certainly consider the possibilities of setting up a plant there. Both Spain and Portugal have an enormous need for foreign capital to finance their development. Direct investment by UK manufacturing companies in local industry is seen as part of this process.

Switzerland

Even the Swiss, although not members of the EC, can hardly avoid the influences of the trend towards greater European integration. Traditionally their financial institutions have attracted large flows of funds from abroad. Their equity markets, however, are structured to prevent foreign investors acquiring ownership influence over their quoted companies. Given that leading Swiss companies remain acquisitive outside their own borders, this kind of imbalance is unlikely to persist. The Swiss are going to find it increasingly difficult to prevent EC companies acquiring strategic holdings in their quoted companies.

Venture capital

Catalytic

The biggest challenge facing the venture capital industry is that it must act as a major catalyst in turning Europe into a genuinely homogeneous home market for all EC companies in the post-1992 era. It is a tall order. If successful, however, the pickings for UK business may be rich indeed. Any start-up business in the USA, particularly in the hi-tech arena where modern concepts of venture capitalism originate, has the considerable advantage of having a large home market in which to sell

Market size

its wares. In the UK any start-up business attempting to tackle all twelve different markets of the EC from the outset would, under present conditions, be regarded as particularly foolhardy.

Yet often, and this applies particularly to hi-tech business, confining the sales of some highly specialised product solely to the UK may not give sufficient market to make the business viable. In the USA, the large home market has enabled a number of businesses in the electronics field, for instance, to achieve stunning exponential growth in the first few years of their existence without the need to take the risks of entering foreign markets.

The achievement of an integrated barrier-free market in the EC similar in size to that in the USA may be a long way off. The reality is that even if 1992 fulfils the highest expectations and all the trade barriers do fall away, there will remain many other barriers of a legal, cultural and even environmental nature which will frustrate a genuine integration of the European market place on the US model. But 1992 is an important step and provides a great opportunity for the UK's venture capital institutions to support UK business's European expansion.

The UK can claim to possess the best developed of such institutions within the EC. The origins of our venture capital industry go back to the formation of 3i by the Government and the banks in the early 1950s. The movement has flourished in recent years because the UK has had a legal, tax and entrepreneurial environment more appropriate to venture capital than virtually any other member state with the possible exception of the Netherlands. Huge resources are now going into venture capital in the UK. Giant financial institutions such as the pension funds of British Coal may eventually earmark as much as 10 per cent of all funds under management to the venture capital market. Venture capital has also for some time been an international business. An estimated 40 per cent to 50 per cent of the finance provided by independent UK venture capital companies is sourced in the USA, and possibly as much as half the venture capital funds raised in France may stem from UK sources.

The Continent   Development of venture capital in other member states is uneven. However, in certain countries – particularly France and to a lesser extent Spain and West Germany – the venture capital movement is developing its own dynamics. The French may only have developed venture capital to a level where the UK was five years ago, but they are moving rapidly and may only take another couple of years to match the UK's scale of activity. France is beginning to untangle its rigid legal and tax climate based on the Napoleonic code which, cynics would say, takes the line that everything is illegal unless you have had specific permission to do it.

The 'do anything' ambience in which the UK's venture capitalists operate is not something that is replicated in other member states. Indeed, the UK venture capitalists have found that if you put venture capital into a legal or fiscal framework, as in the case of the Business Expansion Scheme, it is not necessarily an unalloyed success. The French seem, however, to be adapting to their more constricting framework. France is not short of entrepreneurs nor is it short of the mature private companies which venture capitalists in the UK find have great appeal as investments and which ought to benefit greatly from injections of finance either from the UK or from locally formed venture capital syndicates.

Minority partnerships   In France, well-established UK groups have tended to set up effectively as minority partners with local venture capital managers. This is the most effective way of recognising the need to adapt to local cultures based on the evidence that the best deals are done through local venture capital companies in each member state. It would not do for the UK simply to invade the European venture capital market. Cultural differences will remain so great that sheer weight of money will not get rid of them. US venture capitalists tried to invade the UK in the seventies with mixed results. Quite apart from the cross-border cultural problems, the UK's 130 venture capital organisations do not perform with equal success. About fifty of these organisations, in fact, have a poor track record.

Having said that, the opportunity is there for the venture capital movement to be the agent for great change within the EC. In particular, these organisations do have the potential to rationalise the differences between national cultures rather than simply trying to break down those cultural barriers. There is much evidence that this is the route already being chosen. It is already possible to raise venture capital for suitable projects virtually anywhere in the EC. Partnerships between UK and French venture capital companies are being created and similar links are also being forged in Italy and Spain. In West Germany proposed increases in the rate of capital gains tax from the beginning of 1990 from 28 per cent to 53 per cent have created a tremendous transaction boom in private companies. The tax changes, regarded as a punishment tax on enterprise by many people, are leading to a massive re-structuring of commercial ownership, creating golden opportunities both for UK venture capital funds to invest and for UK corporate entities to acquire privately owned German companies. It is said that in the post-1992 border-free Europe the number of sales of medium-sized business enterprises will double or even triple. West Germany alone may complete 6,000 such deals by 1990.

Venture Consort Scheme

In Brussels, the European Commission itself is in on the act through its Venture Consort Scheme, whereby the Commission and various venture capital partners share the profits on the projects they support. The European Venture Capital Association (EVCA), meanwhile, has begun a campaign urging businesses to ensure that 1992 is an experience to be enjoyed by EC companies rather than just by Japan and the USA. In such a climate it is possible for start-up companies to begin to have a European-wide perspective from the outset. Under the auspices of EVCA, support networks are being set up to help young companies achieve this European view of their businesses. It is a move into uncharted territory in many ways and not helped by the fact that so many deals are now being generated that nearly all venture capitalists are very stretched. And the EC remains quite a minefield for companies making acquisitions as well as for venture funds seeking suitable investments.

Venture capital is a £1 billion business in the UK. That is the estimated scale of the commitment to the equity of companies presently being provided by venture capitalists for all kinds of projects ranging from genuine business start-ups to management buy-outs of large long-established organisations. Even this £1 billion figure understates the scale of the venture capital industry. For the equity capital provided is but the tip of the iceberg of debt required to finance these deals and is often equivalent to as much as six times the equity participation. Venture capital is booming in the UK. Some 130 different organisations ranging from large banks through to quite modest private syndicates offer a service of one kind or another. Three years ago there were perhaps only fifty venture capital companies. In 1980 perhaps only twenty. Ten years earlier only half a dozen. The boom started in the early 1980s and has tended to accelerate in the past two or three years as the entrepreneurial culture created by the Thatcher government takes a firm hold on the UK business community.

Selection

Generally speaking, the larger organisations which offer a venture capital service are looking to invest a minimum of £250,000 in any business proposition. In reality most of the transactions they undertake involve a lot more. Deals involving tens of millions of pounds will mean a venture capital company underwriting a syndicate deal with a number of financial institutions. Typically the initiating bank might invest up to £5 million on its own account while the rest of the syndicate will put up, say, £2 million apiece.

Each venture capital institution has its own rules but normally the banks will not take more than a 30 per cent stake in the company. For a large cross-border deal, no one institution backing it would hold more than 5 per cent of the equity. In the main, the banks look at deals where the profitability of the company is a minimum £150,000 a year. They do, however, look at recovery situations and so-called management buy-ins, where they back a new management team to take control of the company. An organisation like 3i with its long history of involvement in venture capital and its extensive network of regional offices would look at smaller enterprises than this. The banks themselves offer soft loans and options to acquire equity of small growing businesses.

The business plan

The venture capital company will expect the prospective customer to supply a business plan to give it a feel for the capacity of the company and its management and for the nature of its business. It will want a general background and history; a summary of the present state of the business, its finances, trading performance and the state of the markets in which it operates. It will then require three-year projections of profit and loss, cash flow and balance sheets. The assumptions on which these projections are based will need to be spelt out. Also a description of the control systems in place will be required, together with a description of the management and details of the management structure. After all this information has been supplied, the chances are that the venture capitalist will reject the application for new finance. A great many deals are turned down at this stage.

If the applicant clears this first major hurdle, it is likely that the two sides will spend time getting to know each other better. There is plenty of choice of deals and plenty of choice of venture capitalists these days. So it is wise for both sides to be comfortable with one another and feel they can work well together. A decision to go forward is usually preceded by a visit to the company's operation and an **Indicative offer** 'indicative offer' without commitment. This brings in the process of due diligence with an independent accountant's report to supplement investigations by the company's own accountants and lawyers and those of the venture capitalists. An independent accountant's report is a pre-condition of any deal. No two companies have the same financial needs but the cash flow is the key to how a deal is structured and how the interest and dividend payments are staged.

Method of finance Normally the finance comes in a package of ordinary shares, preference shares with special rights, and debt, overdraft and working-capital facilities. The speed with which a deal can be put in place can depend on the ability of the venture capitalist to pass on part of the risk through underwriting to a syndicate of other institutional investors. A very quick deal might be struck inside a month but mostly they take three months to complete.

Venture capitalists do not always make their own appointments to the board of the company they back. Often they draw on lists of independent specialists to act as non-executive directors. However, they naturally expect to be able to attend board meetings and to receive a steady flow of information. Their aim is to see the business on to its next stage of development and to take a capital gain when that happens. It may come through a takeover, a trade sale or sometimes a flotation of the company on the stock market. Sometimes a ratchet mechanism linked to eventual profits achieved is employed to determine the amount of equity the management eventually holds. This means that if the company does better than forecast, the venture capitalist backers wind up with a smaller share of the larger cake but paying the same price. The mechanism can also be made to work in reverse. Normally for cross-border transactions the venture company will take a stake in the parent company, not its overseas subsidiary. Venture capitalists tend to be flexible on fees. For the larger syndicated transaction they might look for 2 per cent of the funds raised. For small deals the fees may be nominal if there are any at all. Essentially they look for a capital gain on the risk they take in backing a business venture.

MBO

This system of financing seems to be working well, particularly in its most recent manifestation: the management buy-out (MBO). The success of this method of transferring ownership of large lumps of the UK's industrial assets derives from its relatively low-risk nature. Few MBOs lead to genuine failure in the sense of loss of equity by the parties. By contrast, perhaps half of all business start-ups fall by the wayside. It is understandable that there is little risk in a well-established business being acquired by those who have managed it for some time already. Certainly it explains why the bulk of the £1 billion of equity finance currently in place has gone into large MBO deals. It is estimated that some 80 per cent of all money has gone into the largest 20 per cent of all the deals, with the high-risk start-up money spread much more thinly around a large number of ventures.

Venture capital is having a dramatic effect on ownership of commerce in the UK. In the course of any day, the stream of corporate news released to the media is likely to include at least three or four deals involving venture capital. It is estimated that of the top 500 UK companies, some seventy or so have been through the venture capital mill in one way or another. The proportion is bound to grow. In the USA it is already 200 companies of the top 500 as the buy-out boom continues.

In the end, success or failure in venture capital for start-ups and immature companies depends on a bond of trust between the entrepreneur and the provider of venture capital finance. A certain level of business morality is required for the system to work and that level will vary from business person to business person.

Eurobond markets

While there may be limits to integration after 1992 in other forms of capital investment, this does not apply in the Eurobond market. This market in terms of corporate debt is already by nature global in its perspective and geographic barriers often count for little.

Eurobonds are similar to bonds issued by companies in domestic money markets, except that they are issued in the Eurocurrency markets. A Eurocurrency is a currency held outside its country of origin; so sterling deposited in a Paris bank is Eurosterling and dollars deposited in London are Eurodollars. The Eurocurrency and Eurobond markets are also known collectively as Euromarkets. There is no single market place, transactions being conducted in financial centres around the world, although London is the main centre, with US, Japanese and UK banks the dominant operators of the markets.

Origins

The Eurocurrency market originated in the late 1950s, but it really took off when the system of fixed exchange rates ended in the 1970s and companies started borrowing and making deposits in Eurocurrencies as a way of protecting themselves against the risk of adverse exchange-rate movements. Eurobonds developed out of Eurocurrencies as lending became increasingly securitised (the bundling of loans into tradeable assets).

Eurobonds are issued by companies (multinationals and the largest corporates only), banks, governments and supranational institutions such as the European Commission to raise long-term finance (five years and more) at competitive interest rates, although recent years have seen the development of a short- to medium-term bond called a

Euronote

Euronote (see pp. 71–2). The advantages of the Eurobond market over domestic markets are its size, which makes it easier and cheaper to raise funds, and its freedom from regulation by governments.

Issue

When a company issues Eurobonds it usually does so in several countries at once through an international syndicate of banks. The most favoured currency for a Eurobond is the dollar, although other stable and fully convertible currencies are used such as sterling, the yen, guilder and Deutschemark. The buyers of Eurobonds – either at the time of issue, or when they are traded in the secondary market – are mainly investment institutions, banks and insurance companies, although wealthy individuals invest in them too.

As a source of funds the Eurobond market is at present only accessible to the largest corporations with the highest credit-ratings. (There are only about twenty-five UK corporations which issue Eurobonds.) A major challenge for 1992 will be to encourage investors to look favourably on a wider range of companies.

An indication of how the trend might develop comes from the Eurosterling convertible bond market, where the range of companies using these instruments has now extended well beyond the largest

Convertible bonds

businesses which use the conventional Eurobond market. 'Convertible' here refers to possible conversion of the bond into the issuer's shares. This is also known as an 'equity sweetener' or 'equity kicker', the intention being to improve the attractiveness of the bond to potential investors.

The Euromarkets remain quality conscious and though demand for their instruments is strong, the investors in this market are by nature highly sophisticated. This market is not a soft option for the borrower, while the cost of financing through Eurobonds may become more expensive as the authorities seek to impose sterner regulations on the market.

However, the number of European banks that might wish to support less well-known UK companies could well increase dramatically in the run up to 1992. This is because many banks wish to become more Europeanised and spread their risk geographically as the barriers to financial services come down. They are becoming more willing to look down the list below the top credit-rated companies in markets with which they are less familiar. In addition, substantial companies which are below the 'first rank' may well achieve acceptability in the Euromarkets through carefully targeted efforts to meet investor requirements. One option is to provide buyers with the possibility of conversion out of debt into equity as might be on offer in the Eurosterling equity convertible market. The challenge facing UK companies in this bracket is to make the European investment community more aware of who they are and what they are doing. The same may apply equally to companies from other member states seeking finance from UK investment institutions. To this end corporate borrowers and their financial advisers may well set up investor relations programmes, embarking on 'European Roadshows' to present to potential investors. This would go hand in hand with other efforts to establish a European-wide vision of their activities. All the signs are that investors will be receptive to such approaches.

Fees

When raising funds in the Eurobond markets the banks basically buy the whole bond issue from the borrower, who gets, for example, proceeds of £98 million from a £100 million issue. The £2 million difference accounts for the complex scale of fees of the participants involved in underwriting the issue. Effectively this means that no fees or charges are passed over until the whole transaction is consummated. Broadly speaking, a five-year bond would be subject to the equivalent of a 1.875 per cent charge, with the fee effectively taken as a selling concession by the underwriting banks' attempting to make an equivalent profit on the bond through the pricing mechanism as it is released to the market. If the bond has an element of equity sweetener or kicker built in, then the banks are likely to charge more. In these cases they usually expect to make the equivalent of between 2.25 per cent and 3 per cent on the transaction.

Usually these factors are all built into the terms of the bond issue. There is in effect an 'all-in-cost' of raising the funds, which covers fees and expenses and is reflected in the price. The cheapest terms are not necessarily always the best, since the issuing company may well need to return to the Eurobond market again. If the previous issue did not go too well because it was not sufficiently attractively priced either for the underwriting banks or for the investors, there may be problems in re-entering the market.

15. Case studies

Many of the financial techniques, products and services described in the previous chapters can, at times, be difficult to envisage in their practical business context. This is where case studies come in useful. Real examples of how firms have financed their EC strategies provide a clearer understanding of the subject: of the real-life problems that can be encountered, and how they can be surmounted.

This concluding chapter profiles four UK companies which have used various types and levels of finance, either to sell goods or services in the EC, or to establish a physical presence there. B&W Loudspeakers used factoring services to boost speaker sales to West Germany; Bayswater Tubes and Sections used forfaiting to sell aluminium tubes to France; Queens Moat Houses negotiated a £415 million multi-option facility to finance hotel acquisitions in West Germany and the Netherlands; while British Vita – a major force in foam rubber, fibres and polymer compounds – paid for a string of European acquisitions by using local banks to raise working capital in local currency, and UK banks to raise medium-term currency loans.

Even for those who have a good understanding of trade-related finance, these case studies make informative reading in that they illustrate in detail what actually happens when firms seek to raise new forms of finance.

B&W Loudspeakers

Late payments by overseas distributors provided the impetus for B&W Loudspeakers to turn to factoring as a solution. The company, which manufactures high quality hi-fi loudspeakers in Worthing, Sussex, exports about 90 per cent of its annual £12 million turnover, the bulk of it to other members states. Since it was established in 1965, it has twice won the Queen's Award for Export Achievement.

These days, 85 per cent of its turnover – almost all of its exports – is handled by a factoring company. B&W decided to use factoring services in the early 1970s, when its North American distributor got into cash-flow difficulties and asked for longer credit terms. B&W found it difficult to meet this request. The problem was that, at a time when sales were increasing at a healthy rate, too much of B&W's working capital was already tied up waiting for receivables from its distributors in other countries. Even though the company had always been prudently run (dividends had never been paid and all the profits of the business had been retained), there was still insufficient liquidity to finance debtors.

An obvious option for B&W was to ask its bank for finance, in the form of an overdraft, for example. This, however, would not have overcome the two major problems B&W faced – too much capital tied up in receivables, and the difficulty of collecting debts from geographically distant debtors. So it approached the factoring subsidiary of its clearing bank, and found the solution. The factor took over B&W's debtor book, providing pre-payments to B&W on its invoices and taking responsibility for collecting the debts. The key point was that B&W got valuable working capital to bridge the gap between invoicing and receiving payment.

Keith Anderson, Finance Director of B&W, says: 'In many quarters of the UK, turning to a factor is seen as one step from insolvency. This was far from the case for B&W. We were not "fire-fighting" but trying instead to make the best use of our working capital to support our growth strategy. Although bad debts had never been a real problem, the bad-debt protection afforded under the factoring arrangement was a comfort. It took away one area of concern in our cyclical industry.' He says that his overseas distributors have never been put off by having to deal with a factor. On the contrary, it seems to have raised the level of trading confidence in its export business all round, in addition to leaving B&W adequately funded.

In 1987, B&W decided there would be benefits in taking a controlling interest in its West German distributor, who was suffering increasing cash-flow problems, despite strong management. B&W was able to do this because the UK factor, with offices in West Germany, agreed to take control of the distributor's debtor book. However, the factor has now worked itself out of a job! The German distributor has become highly liquid, and the factoring arrangement has been terminated.

Anderson thinks that, in a financial sense, B&W could dispense with factoring entirely, but that the benefit in costs saved would be marginal. 'Moreover, we rather like the arrangement of having a third party to police our debtors,' he says. 'We also know that there may come a time in the business cycle when the support of our factoring company, with whom we have built up a relationship of trust and confidence, will smooth our passage through difficult times.'

Bayswater Tubes & Sections Limited

A decade after being the subject of a management buy-out from Alcoa, one of the UK's three leading aluminium welded tube producers, Bayswater Tubes and Sections has firmly established itself in South Wales as a manufacturer of aluminium tube for use in everything from orthopaedic equipment to ladders and garden chairs. The management team, led by Chairman William Kirkup and his son Peter, who is Managing Director, has managed to quadruple sales since buying their independence and, following a successful initial foray into France, has identified Europe as an area for future growth.

Expansion from its base at Pencoed first began at the end of 1987 when Bayswater saw an opportunity in France following the closure of the main French aluminium welded tube manufacturer. That led Finance Director Wayne Jones to look closely at the ways in which this move could be financed. 'It could be financed by such means as letters of credit and so on but, after looking at all the options, we took the advice of our local bank manager and decided to opt for forfaiting as the best way of doing this.'

Forfaiting is the means by which a bank can give up to 100 per cent finance to a company that supplies either goods or services in the UK or abroad where credit terms are sought between ninety days and five years or more. In a forfaiting transaction, the bank effectively buys the bill of exchange or other types of debt instrument which the exporting company receives in return for the goods it is supplying. Since the UK bank takes over all the commercial, political, currency and transfer risks, it will normally demand that the bills of exchange are avalised or guaranteed by the importer's local bank. In those instances where the bank is able to credit-assess the buyer's balance sheet, the need for an aval may not arise. Indeed, Bayswater asked for the aval to be omitted in the case of their French buyers to speed up payment and also to reduce the buyer's costs.

'Forfaiting couldn't be simpler,' explains Mr Wayne Jones. 'We get the goods ready, they are exported to France and then a bill of exchange is sent back. We send that to our bank in London and the following day payment is made to our local branch in Pencoed.'

Bayswater is currently exporting two 20-tonne loads of aluminium tubes a month to France, for use in ladders and television aerials. That already means sales of around £70,000 per month, with the group planning to increase its volume of exports significantly. 'What forfaiting has meant is that we have been able to expand our sales into Europe far faster than we would otherwise have been able to do,' says Wayne Jones.

Almost 25 per cent of the group's annual turnover of £3 million is now accounted for by exports to France and the success of that move has already prompted Bayswater – which has a forty-two-strong workforce – to look at the Dutch, Scandinavian and West German markets. The Bayswater board has no plans to go public but is looking at diversification into related products and manufacturing processes.

Wayne Jones's advice to other small companies with an eye on Europe is: 'Make sure you have tied up a clearly worded contract with your Continental customers. Secondly, talk to your bank about financing options, bearing in mind that Continental customers normally want longer credit terms than is customary in the UK.'

Queens Moat Houses PLC

Lack of suitable acquisition opportunities in the UK has been the main driving force behind an aggressive European expansion programme at Queens Moat Houses, the hotel chain chaired by John Bairstow. A series of deals in West Germany and the Benelux countries has transformed the group to the point where half its hotel rooms are now outside the UK, and half its total earnings in the current year will come from Continental hotels.

'It all started in 1986 when we bought the Bilderberg chain of hotels in Holland,' explains Deputy Chairman, Martin Marcus. 'That set us up in Holland at a time when we were looking at the Continent, since finding suitable UK hotels was getting extremely difficult.'

To date, Queens Moat has spent almost £300 million to establish itself as the biggest hotel operator in West Germany, where it has 4,500 rooms, and the biggest hotelier in the Netherlands, where its hotels have a combined total of some 1,800 rooms. Buying hotels in Europe is proving a far more cost-effective exercise than adding to the seventy-two strong UK chain, since purchase costs are substantially less. In its latest £96 million deal to buy seven Crest Hotels from Bass, the cost per bedroom worked out at less than £75,000. 'That deal included rooms in the centre of Frankfurt, and we would simply not be able to buy space in a place like the centre of Manchester,' says Marcus. 'There is no market to judge what the price in Manchester might be, but it could well be £150,000 a room or more.'

Queens Moat was fortunate in picking up a head office in the Netherlands through its Bilderberg acquisition and was able to establish an administrative base in West Germany when it acquired the former Holiday Inns head office.

Owning only twenty-seven hotels in West Germany, the group sees considerable scope both for further acquisitions and for substantial development and upgrading of its existing portfolio: 'I cannot see us having as many hotels in West Germany as we have in the UK, but we could double the present number without overstretching our head office,' says Marcus. 'West Germany has the strongest economy in Europe, a very low inflation rate and a very solid interest-rate policy.'

But the date of 1992, says Marcus, does not figure strongly in the group's thinking, adding that the group has its eye on the Channel

Tunnel opening in 1993 through its interest in a hotel being built in Kent. The 200-bed Ashford International Hotel is due to open in March 1990, and promises to be the first top-class hotel to be completed in time for the town's future role as the major commercial and transport centre on the UK side of the Channel. It is being financed largely through a Business Expansion Scheme, although Queens Moat will have an eventual 24 per cent stake in the development in addition to a management contract to run the hotel.

Finance for the last three years of European expansion has been consolidated in the form of a £415 million multi-option facility provided by a consortium of banks in London. Under this facility, Queens Moat Houses is able to borrow in various currencies, including Deutschemarks and guilders. With the assistance of its UK-based lender banks, the company has thus financed its West German and Dutch acquisitions in local currency without need for negotiation with lenders in Frankfurt or Amsterdam. Having an income-flow in these currencies, the company has a natural hedge against exposure to future exchange- and interest-rate movements.

The company's cash resources and shareholders' funds have been bolstered by a series of rights issues, the latest of which was successfully completed in October 1988, raising £57.5 million. This reflected the company's prudent approach to borrowed funds, the directors considering it inappropriate to undertake their programme of expansion on borrowed money alone.

British Vita PLC

Acquisitions in Europe have helped transform Manchester-based British Vita into a major force in the world of foam rubber, fibres and polymer compounds, and it is expected to notch up sales in the current year of some £550 million.

Over the last couple of years, British Vita has spent almost £50 million in broadening the scope of its business, and turning what was largely a UK and Commonwealth business into one in which almost 60 per cent of turnover now comes from its European operations. British Vita has proved the wisdom of its aggressive expansion to the stock-market through a steady increase in profits from £12.5 million in 1985 to £28.3 million in 1987, and the City is expecting a total of around £36 million for 1988.

The overall strategy is centred upon building up a broadly based business, supplying specialised components for a wide range of industries ranging from transportation and furniture to packaging, filtration and the leisure industry. However, far from being a financial conglomerate, the common link in all Vita's businesses is polymer technology, which gives the company its slogan – 'The Magical World of Polymers'.

The company philosophy is strongly based on a de-centralised management having total profit and financial responsibility for their individual product/market areas, and growth often emanates from both organic and acquisition ideas generated within these business units. Tighter rules on foam- and fibre-filled furniture have recently given a major boost to British Vita in the UK because the Vita business units involved were in the forefront of developing the technology to produce filling which met the new safety standards.

'Our main drive into Europe started back in 1984,' explains Finance Director Rod Sellers. 'That was when we decided to re-orientate our business away from a major presence in Africa and concluded that Europe offered us the chance to acquire companies which were relatively cheap to buy and offered scope for growth.' Sellers points out that most European countries do not have such developed capital markets as the UK, which means European management does not have ready access to such options as management or leveraged buy-outs, nor can it readily find backing from an equivalent of the UK's Unlisted Securities Market. 'We picked up several companies which were part of larger groupings and which had gone a little bit downstream into a position where they were finding that the rigid disciplines of a big parent company were not suitable to the development of the business. That gave us the opportunity to acquire them at a relatively modest price, but meant we had to invest time and money in re-orientating the management into looking at themselves as an individual profit centre, rather than as functional executives within a larger organisation.'

The European expansion was in technical and product areas with which British Vita was already familiar and so the only real hurdles were the different languages and cultures throughout Europe. However, British Vita's history of working with partners in very different economies assisted them in rapidly recognising and overcoming these problems, which, to other UK acquiring companies, often appear insuperable.

Local managers in the new Vita companies could be persuaded that the company had a real interest in their business and, by harnessing the joint efforts of all concerned, that the motivation behind Vita's acquisition was to generate growth rather than asset strip. The emphasis on creating an environment in which teamwork can produce positive results has been a feature of Vita's management style and, in their opinion, while it does not perhaps produce immediate short-term benefits, it creates a much better basis for the companies to develop over the medium term. 'We found Europeans were not used to the profit-centre-manager concept, and were bottom-line conscious. That meant a lot of effort persuading them they should be proud of making profits rather than just servicing all the various people who depended on the company for a livelihood.'

To pay for this string of acquisitions, Sellers has learnt the value of bringing in a locally based bank alongside one of the UK clearing banks. He also has a policy of borrowing in the local currency as a means of hedging any currency risk. 'Our policy is normally to use a major local bank for working capital and for establishing our credibility in the particular country, while backing that up with medium-term currency loans and one of our major corporate relationship banks, NatWest, Lloyds and Deutsche.'

Appendix 1: Banking systems in the EC

The similarities between the banking systems in the EC are more striking than the differences. Although the lawyers will be busy even after the 1992 deadline, the majority of the member states will have little difficulty in bringing their banking practices into line with EC directives.

The major difficulties will be faced by countries such as Greece, Portugal and Denmark, where much remains to be done to make their domestic banks competitive with the internationally known banks of West Germany, France and the UK.

Recent developments in the UK bank sector reflect changes that have been going on throughout the Community. In almost every instance there has been a consolidation of banking activity as the traditional boundaries between the different types of credit institution become blurred. These institutions believe that 1992 will create a greater demand for 'one-stop' banking, that companies benefiting from the growth of the European market will want their prime relationship banks to provide a full range of services in every member state.

The 1987 Banking Act helped the process of simplification by replacing traditional definitions of a bank with the term 'authorised institution'. The UK clearing banks have added to their traditional role as providers of short-term credit and have begun to offer medium- to long-term finance. The clearers have moved into mortgage lending, while the building societies have developed personal banking services.

Belgium

Banking activity is overseen by a number of regulatory bodies, the main monetary bodies being the Ministry of Finance, the National Bank of Belgium and the Belgo-Luxembourg Exchange Institute. The main regulator of banking activity is the Banking Commission, which oversees bank solvency and the activities of the three main forms of credit institutions: the deposit banks, public credit institutions and the private savings banks.

The basic legislation affecting banking is the Royal Decree of July 1935, which set out to split up large credit institutions into separate entities. In effect, many of the largest banks were divided into a deposit bank and a holding company. This has since been amended in a number of laws. The most recent, in 1985, brought Belgian banking law in line with the EC directives.

Banks are prohibited from holding shares in industrial or commercial companies, except in specific (and rare) instances. Although there have been modifications to the original law, it has been made clear that banks may hold shares only as investments and may not exert influence over the management of the companies.

Denmark

Of all the member states in the EC, Denmark may see its banking system altered the most radically by 1992. The current debate in Copenhagen is about the effect of the government's proposal (set out in a White Paper of 1987) to change the way the capital adequacy ratio is calculated. Currently it is an unweighted calculation based on a bank's liabilities. The government's proposal is to switch the emphasis to the asset side of the balance sheet – the net effect being to make domestic requirements higher than the 8 per cent ratio set out in the Second Banking Directive.

Danish banks already face more stringent capital adequacy requirements than other EC banks. Even so, it has been suggested that some of the smaller banks may well look for mergers with foreign institutions to escape the domestic legislation.

Denmark has inherited a banking system designed to service an agricultural society. Though the numerous small local and regional banks are being gradually absorbed into national networks, the competition for business is still fierce. Because the market is over-banked, some US banks have closed their Copenhagen operations.

There are three main types of credit institution:

- Commercial banks. These are universal banks offering the full range of credit and investment services. They are, however, prohibited from exercising control over commercial and industrial enterprises.

- Savings banks, which will shortly be allowed to issue capital on the stock market, are allowed to take deposits and to lend, though the majority of their business is in the retail sector.

- Mortgage credit institutions. These provide the majority of building loans, raising funds on the domestic bond market. In addition, two special institutions provide industrial and shipping finance. The commercial banks have never sought to challenge the mortgage banks' strength in mortgage finance. This could be one area where foreign banks will be able to attract domestic customers.

Supervision of banking activity is carried out by a special department of the Ministry of Industry. Monetary authority resides with the Danmarks Nationalbank.

Overdrafts, both secured and unsecured, to commercial borrowers are the most important form of short-term lending by Danish banks. The importance of international trade to Denmark means that Danish banks have developed an extensive system of direct foreign currency loans for corporate borrowers.

France

Banking in France has been the subject (some would say the victim) of intervention by successive governments. In 1982, thirty-nine banks were nationalised, bringing more than 90 per cent of the retail banking sector under government control. Within four years another government had embarked on a course of bank privatisation, only for the programme to be stopped in 1988. The emphasis is now on the creation of multi-purpose institutions able to compete with competition from West Germany, Benelux and the UK.

Until the 1960s, French banks were structured into three distinct groups, deposit banks, investment banks and long-term credit institutions. The basic aim of the legislation was to ensure that French industry was provided with a ready supply of finance. The various reforms since 1966, culminating in the 1984 Banking Reform Act, have gradually removed the distinctions. There is still evidence of these divisions, especially as companies tend to have relationships with many banks to ensure a wide supply of credit facilities.

Under the 1984 Act supervision of banking activity was entrusted to no less than four bodies, the National Credit Council (CNC), the Banking Regulation Committee (CRB), the Credit Establishment

Committee (CEC), and the Banking Commission, though the effective control of the system is in the hands of the Banque de France. The savings bank system is controlled by the Caisse des Dépôts et Consignations, which acts as both a central deposit agency and as a government investment agency.

Until the 1984 Act, the monetary authorities exerted very tight credit controls. Now France has fallen into line with most other member states, with interest rates being the main instrument of monetary policy. Although very short-term loans and overdrafts are available, the discount of trade paper remains the most used form of short-term financing. Bills are often tied to the specific purpose of the loan.

Greece

The banking system in Greece is arguably the weakest in the Community. The heavy involvement of the Greek state in almost every aspect of finance is going to make it difficult to achieve a competitive banking system by 1992.

Among the commercial banks, the National Bank of Greece and the Commercial Bank of Greece account for the vast majority of deposit taking and lending. Both of these institutions are owned by public sector bodies. The three major investment banks, the Hellenic Industrial Development Bank, the National Bank of Industrial Development and the Investment Bank, the country's major providers of long-term credit, are effectively under state control.

There are some signs of change. The Bank of Greece is gradually relaxing its traditionally tight hold on banking practice. Greek banks are now free to lend for working capital without reference to the central bank. Until 1984, overdraft facilities were illegal but since then this form of lending has grown rapidly. Now the most common form of short-term finance is an overdraft, with fluctuations within an agreed limit. Banks are now free to quote their own interest rates for drachmas, subject to Bank of Greece minima. Banks may also lend foreign currency to companies operating in Greece, in which case the interest rate is freely negotiable, subject to Bank of Greece maxima.

Italy

Italy has inherited a highly regionalised banking system made up of more than 1,100 commercial banks with a total of 13,000 branches. Yet despite the diversity, banking in Italy is tightly controlled by the state. Banking activity is overseen by the Treasury minister, the Bank of Italy and the Interministry Committee for Credit and Savings (CICR). The powers exercised by these authorities are wide ranging, covering everything from banking fees to the credit limits that a bank may set for any one customer.

In addition to tight regulatory control, the state has effective ownership of three 'banks of national interest' and the six 'public law banking institutions', which dominate the banking sector in terms of size.

Until recently, Italy maintained a distinction between 'ordinary credit institutions', permitted to take deposits and offer short-term loans, and providers of medium- or long-term loans (of over eighteen months) such as public law banks. The only way around the restriction for the commercial banks was through the creation of separate medium- and long-term lending institutions for this purpose, usually in partnership with other banks.

Given this highly involved structure it is easy to see that 1992 is going to lead to a major shake-up of the banking sector. From 15 December 1989, banks need only comply with EC guidelines to be granted bank status and need no longer subject themselves to the elaborate criteria set out by the CICR.

Short-term finance is usually provided by fairly simple credit lines. Unsecured overdraft facilities are available but are generally offered only to customers with the highest creditworthiness. In the past, interest rates charged to borrowers have been at a substantial premium to the effective base rate. This reflected the high level of compulsory deposits that the banks are required to make with the central bank. One effect of 1992 already being felt is greater competition in the cost of borrowing.

Luxembourg

The Grand Duchy of Luxembourg has by far the most unusual finance system in the Community. The tiny domestic economy means that domestic banking is far less important than international finance activities. The real question facing Luxembourg is what effect the harmonisation of the bank disclosure and tax legislation by 1992 will have. Private banking for foreign residents is one of the pillars of banking in the Duchy. If the secrecy and tax advantages of these accounts were threatened, there could a flight of capital to Switzerland and other 'offshore' centres.

The regulation of banking is overseen by the Luxembourg Monetary Institute. The monetary union with Belgium means that the government's ability to control monetary policy is limited. While there is no central bank, the Caisse d'Épargne de l'État acts as the state's banker and operates the national clearing system. The Caisse is also the most active provider of medium- and long-term credit to local businesses and individuals.

The majority of domestic banking activity is controlled by the 'local banks', Banque International à Luxembourg, Banque Générale du Luxembourg and Kredietbank Luxembourgeoise. Each of these is closely linked to a major Belgian bank.

Short-term finance is dominated by short-term loans and overdrafts with minimum interest rates set by the Association des Banques et Banquiers Luxembourgeois. Because the Caisse d'Épargne does not have extensive rediscounting facilities, discounting of bills and trade paper is a rarely used option.

The Netherlands

Though Dutch banks seem to be following the general European pattern of becoming full service institutions, three distinct types of banking remain:

- Commercial banks, offering the same range of services as the major UK clearing banks. The two largest, Algemene Bank Nederland and Amsterdam–Rotterdam Bank (AMRO), account for nearly two-thirds of the sector's assets. The movement towards full-service banking was highlighted by the co-operation agreement between AMRO and Belgium's Générale Bank, which could lead to partial or total integration.

- Rabobanks, originally set up as agricultural credit institutions. They have now expanded their commercial banking operations, increasing their share of lending to medium and large corporations.

- Savings banks, which are regionally based savings institutions, although they now offer most of the retail banking services. In this group is the state-owned Postbank. This was formed from the merger of the Post Office Savings Bank and the Postal and Giro Service. Postbank has been remodelled gradually. From simple savings accounts it has moved into mortgage and consumer lending and is now offering a full range of banking services to corporate as well as retail customers.

De Nederlandsche Bank, the Dutch central bank, is both the bank regulator and the monetary authority. Overdrafts are the most often used form of short-term lending to business. Larger corporate customers often cover short-term requirements with a fixed-rate loan, usually with a one- to three-month maturity. This kind of loan is generally cheaper than an overdraft, reflecting the greater creditworthiness of borrowers.

Portugal

Portugal's turbulent political history has left its mark on the country's financial system. In 1975 the commercial banks were nationalised and reorganised and the resulting nine publicly owned institutions now dominate banking activity. The other types of credit institution are:

- Private commercial banks: since 1984 nine commercial banks have been set up, six of them foreign owned. Though they cannot match their public counterparts in terms of branch networks, they have been successful in the growing corporate banking sector.

- Savings banks: these were not nationalised in 1975 and are restricted in their lending activities. In addition to the private institutions there are also the Caixa Geral de Depositos and the Post Office Savings System.

- Investment banks, concentrating on medium- to long-term credit

EC membership has had a beneficial effect on banking in Portugal. It lay behind the encouragement of private sector and foreign banks and forced the government to adopt a deposit guarantee scheme. Yet much remains to be done to improve the competitiveness of domestic banks. For example, central government still operates strict credit limits on individual institutions. It seems unlikely that Portuguese banks will be able to compete in the post-1992 financial services market without joint ventures with foreign institutions.

The Republic of Ireland

The banking system in the Republic of Ireland did not develop fully until the late 1960s. Before then, Ireland relied heavily on the UK banks. The demand for finance from a rapidly growing industrial sector led to the Central Bank Act 1971, which put the regulation of the Irish banking system firmly under the control of the Central Bank of Ireland.

In 1979 the Republic of Ireland joined the EMS, ending the direct links between the Irish punt and sterling. In effect it ended the country's dependence on the UK for monetary policy and increased the importance of the Central Bank's role. The Irish government has also been keen to promote Dublin as a financial centre, and has offered major tax incentives to foreign companies establishing operations in Dublin.

The main types of banks are:

- The associated banks, which correspond to the main clearing banks in the UK. There are four dominant institutions: Allied Irish Banks, the Bank of Ireland, Ulster Bank and Northern Bank. The last two are foreign owned. The associated banks have by far the largest branch networks.

- Falling under the same basic legislation as the associated banks are a range of institutions specialising in commercial and investment banking, corresponding to the specialist banks in the City of London.

- Savings banks: this sector consists of the state-organised Post Office Savings Bank and Trustee Savings Bank (not to be confused with the UK institution) which operate savings schemes for retail investors.

- Building societies, organised on the same lines as their UK counterparts.

Most short-term lending is in the form of overdrafts and direct loans. The rates of interest charged depend on the size and creditworthiness of the borrower. Thought less often used, other forms of finance such as the discounting of trade paper are readily available.

Spain

The recent history of Spanish banking has been dominated by a series of mergers and takeovers that have slowly drawn together a hitherto highly regionalised banking system.

Following a series of banking crises, which saw the central Bank of

Spain bail out almost half the nation's banks, there has been a liberalisation of rules on foreign ownership of banks and the introduction, in 1977, of a deposit guarantee scheme. Many foreign observers still feel that there is a lack of sophistication in Spanish finance.

The Banking Law of 1962 separated the commercial and investment banking activities to prevent short-term deposits from being used for long-term finance. A series of reforms has now removed the legal distinctions between most forms of banking activity, though there is still a large degree of specialisation between the commercial, investment and savings banks.

Banking is dominated by the privately owned banks which account for around two-thirds of all business lending. In turn, the private commercial banking sector is dominated by seven major institutions.

Over the past two years banks have been keen to promote overdraft finance, with interest linked to preferential rates rather than to the base rate. This is a fairly uncommon technique in Spain and there is still a heavy reliance on the discounting of 30- to 180-day paper and on direct short-term cash loans.

West Germany

West German banks are divided into two principal groups: universal and specialist banks. The corporate banking sector is dominated by the big three universal banks, Deutsche Bank, Dresdner Bank and Commerzbank. These banks offer the full range of banking and financial services, from mortgage lending to stockbroking. In the past the larger universal banks have concentrated on corporate banking activities, leaving the specialists, such as the savings banks and mortgage banks, to develop the retail sector, although there is now a greater overlap of interests.

With nearly all the large German banks, a substantial proportion of their assets (typically 50 to 70 per cent) is represented by mortgage lending funded by bond issues. Another characteristic is the relatively high provision against Less-Developed Country debt, in comparison with European and US competitors.

The size and financial strength of the main German banks has led most observers to conclude that they will emerge as a dominant force in banking across the Community after 1992. Unlike most EC banks, the universals have very significant holdings in German industry and are represented on the boards of many of the largest corporations. The close relationship reflects in part the use of loan capital rather than the capital markets for long-term finance. For that reason, although many foreign banks have established active subsidiaries in West Germany, few have penetrated the domestic market.

In the retail sector, overdrafts are the most commonly used form of short-term financing; although the most expensive, they are the most flexible financing tool for small and medium-sized companies. Larger corporates, however, avail themselves of a host of short- to medium-term money-market facilities in the form of advances, ranging from overnight call money to medium-term maturities. Although this method is less flexible, these borrowings are significantly cheaper. Discounting, the cheapest form of short-term finance, is widely used. The West German Central Bank, the Bundesbank, allocates rediscount limits for individual banks. As German interest rates have fallen, corporate borrowers have been looking to secure medium-term fixed-rate loans in order to lock in cheaper borrowing.

Appendix 2: Legislative impact on banks and the financial sector

Banking directives

The Second Banking Directive is the proposed foundation for the banking and related credit institutions under the EC's 1992 programme. It has its foundations in the First Banking Directive which set out to establish minimum standards for regulating banks and was adopted by the Council in December 1977. The First Banking Directive laid the foundations whereby a credit institution (one that takes deposits and lends money) must have separate and minimum own funds and have at least two directors with reputable management experience. It also stipulated capital requirements without specifying them.

The Second Directive lays down a minimum 5 million ecu capital base below which a bank may not fall. The question of capital is the subject of a separate proposal known as Own Funds which, with the Solvency Ratio Directive, go in tandem with the Second Banking Directive.

Own Funds Proposal

The Own Funds Proposal (on which a common position was agreed in December 1988) follows broadly the international capital adequacy standards laid down by the Basel Committee of the 'Group of 10' nations. The non-G10 members of the EC – Denmark, the Republic of Ireland, Portugal, Greece and Spain – were still not party to the Basel proposals. The Own Funds Proposal also defines types of capital to be used as the numerator for solvency ratios. It is likely that the

Solvency Ratio Proposal

Solvency Ratio Proposal will follow closely those from the Basel Committee. It will set risk-asset weightings for on- and off-balance-sheet assets, which will add up to provide the denominator for the solvency ratio.

Licence

Probably one of the most important principles of the Second Banking Directive is the stipulation that once a credit institution is authorised by its home supervisor, that is, the central bank, it will have a 'passport' to sell its products across the EC. This will also apply to the Mortgage Credit and Investment Services Directives. Banks

143

will not have to queue up for a licence from a central bank in each host country. However, those that are selling a wide range of products which include consumer credit, savings and mortgages will still have to comply with local investor protection and other 'public good' laws. In addition, the proposed Directive lays down that member states may not discriminate against foreign entrants. It also brings in rules for scrutinising large shareholders and includes a highly controversial clause on reciprocity (see p. 10). It sets out additional articles on accounting and control standards.

The important part of the Second Banking Directive for the business sector is that which lays down what business banks may do and offer their clients. The activities permitted are:

- Deposit taking and other forms of borrowing.

- Lending, including consumer credit, mortgages, factoring, trade finance and forfaiting.

- Payment cards, debit cards, electronic funds transfer at point of sale (EFTPOS), travellers cheques and bankers drafts.

- Banks will also be entitled to run credit reference and safe custody services.

- Money broking.

- Leasing.

- Money transmission.

- Guarantees and commitments.

- Trading on own account or for customers in money-market instruments, foreign exchange, financial futures and options, exchange- and interest-rate instruments and securities. They may also take part in the issuing of shares, bonds and other securities.

- The safekeeping of securities.

- The door will be opened to a wide range of corporate advisory services plus taking part in and arranging mergers and acquisitions.

- Portfolio management and advice.

Mortgage credit

There is some controversy over whether the mortgage credit operations of banks and building societies should be absorbed into the

Second Banking Directive as they have been, or whether they should be covered under the separate Mortgage Credit Directive. The Second Banking Directive will give credit institutions providing mortgage credit the 'passport' to operate throughout the EC; the Mortgage Credit Directive will cover the financial techniques used in lending and funding. This is intended to allow the institutions to use the same techniques in the host country that apply in their home country.

Mortgage bonds

A further directive to cover mortgage bonds (a common financing method in West Germany and Denmark) has been shelved until the Second Banking Directive and the Mortgage Credit Directive are resolved.

In principle, the Commission believes this to be one of the most important elements of the long-term goal of financial integration but it has rather shied away from the extreme complexity of trying to harmonise different national systems and laws. It accepts that mortgage lending across borders would give customers a substantially greater choice of mortgage products. It would also allow a variety of investment instruments to fund those products. What appeals to the Commission is that this would heighten competition and so lower the cost of credit and provide a higher return on investors' money.

Bank branch accounts

This somewhat controversial proposal is due to be enforced by 31 December 1990. In effect it reduces public scrutiny of the branch's activities in the host country because it abolishes the right of countries to insist on the publication of separate branch accounts where the parent is licensed through another member state. They have to be consolidated and accounts have to be lodged with local registries of the home state, such as Companies House in the UK. They must also be produced to the host-state authority if requested. There are questions being raised about legalising this reduced disclosure. Some banks may convert their subsidiaries in other member states to branch status to take advantage of this relaxation.

Accounts of banks

This is to be the subject of a major directive to harmonise the Community's company law programme. The accounts for credit institutions are being treated separately from those of other companies.

The main features of the Directive relating to accounts of banks are:

- The law will apply to all acounts for the financial year beginning 1 January 1993

- Banks' trading securities portfolios will have to be reported at current value as well as historic cost

- Concealed reserves will be allowed up to 4 per cent and possibly 5 per cent of some specified assets

- Forward positions will have to be disclosed in notes to the accounts

The control and monitoring of banks and their accounts is the subject of the Consolidated Supervision Directive, which is one of the very few already in force in all twelve member states. Adopted in June 1983, it lays down the need for a supervisor (such as a central bank) to assess the exposure, management and accounts of a bank on a consolidated basis. The Branch Accounts Directive when enforced in 1990 is expected to run in tandem with Consolidated Supervision.

Recommendations

Not everything emanating from Brussels has or will have the force of law behind it. The Commission issues recommendations and although members are not legally bound by them, they do have substantial influence. Some may form the basis of future directives.

Large exposures

In 1987 the Commission issued a recommendation with regard to large exposures, which sets out guidance and limits on exposures to a variety of categories of borrower.

Deposit guarantee

Another recommendation which could form the foundation of a future directive concerns a deposit guarantee scheme already in existence in most member states. The Republic of Ireland introduced its scheme in 1989, Denmark plans to do so by 1 January 1990 and Greece some time after that.

There is also a clause which makes countries with deposit guarantee schemes extend them to countries which do not have them but are host to their bank branches.

Winding up

A related issue is that concerning the winding up or rescuing of a branch. Some countries have not felt such a directive to be necessary and so the draft has not gone before the Council. The proposal is that any winding up should take place according to home-country rules.

EFTPOS

Probably the most important recommendation to come out in the financial services sector concerns electronic payments. It is an issue with potentially huge commercial implications.

Debit

The recommendation is to establish an EC code of conduct for electronic funds transfer at the point of sale (EFTPOS) involving debit, although *not* credit or cheque cards. The recommendation tries to formalise the relationship between financial institutions, traders, the service industry and customers. The Commission's hope is to have by 1992 a system whereby traders and customers can all join the network of their choice by using just one multi-card terminal. It attempts to tackle the confidentiality question and a committee is at present working on standardising the technology, although it will have to overcome potential obstacles in areas of data protection and competition.

Securities

There are several EC directives and proposals concerned with the broad definition of securities. However, the central piece of legislation – the Investment Services Directive – has, at the time of writing, been submitted to the Council. The purpose of the exercise is to provide a directive which will work on the same principle as the Second Banking Directive, doing for investment services firms what the Banking Directive did for credit institutions. It will specify minimum authorisation standards for home countries to apply. Meanwhile a separate Capital Adequacy Directive is expected which will spell out minimum criteria for financial resources plus other aspects already included in the UK's Financial Services Act, including:

- Counterparty risk

- Compensation

- Client money segregation

Banks already authorised under the Second Banking Directive will not have to be authorised additionally under the Investment Services Directive, although it is probable that their conduct of business in the field of securities will fall within its jurisdiction.

Activities expected to fall within the ambit of the Investment Services Directive include:

- Dealing in securities as a principal

- Market making

- Brokerage

- Providing investment advice for a fee

- Portfolio management

- The safekeeping of securities

- The underwriting and distribution of public issues

- Dealing or arranging deals in precious metals

- Trading or arranging deals in financial futures or options on securities and/or precious metals

- Trading or providing customer services in exchange-rate and interest-rate instruments

The Commission's intention is that a common position will be reached by the end of 1989 and that the Directive will be implemented by 1 January 1993.

The rest of the securities industry is subject to a variety of directives on stock exchange activity, transferable securities, taxation, prospectuses, large shareholder disclosure and insider trading.

Admissions Directive

The Admissions Directive, the first of three and already enforced in most countries, sets out to create minimum standards for company listings on stock exchanges. It excludes managed, pooled and closed-end funds and government securities.

This Directive is important to the business community as companies obtaining a quotation on the official stock exchange of one member state will automatically be eligible to be listed on the stock exchanges throughout the Community.

Listing Particulars Directive

The standards to be followed in providing information to stock exchanges are laid out in the Listing Particulars Directive; minimum standards for interim (first six months) reports of listed companies are set out in the Interim Reports Directive.

Securities transaction tax

This is a proposal to abolish indirect taxes on securities transactions which in effect means abolishing stamp duties and stamp-duty reserve tax. The implications for the UK could be profound – in the year to March 1987 stamp duty yielded £1.8 billion to the Exchequer. The proposal will not affect member states' rights to levy capital duty and it does not apply to VAT on commissions. Expected enforcement throughout the Community is 1 October 1989.

Prospectus Proposal

This Proposal, which has now been agreed, aims to harmonise rules for the publishing, scrutiny and distribution of public offers. The Proposal is comprehensive, demanding full information on the condition of a company.

There are exemptions for those already listed on a Community exchange. They are:

- Issues concerned with mergers and acquisitions

- Conversions

- Warrants – both the exercising and substitution of them

- Free issues

- Constantly issued securities such as commercial paper

- Eurobonds in certain circumstances

- Government and local authority debt securities

- Employee issues

- Where a new issue is less than 10 per cent in quantity or value of securities already listed in that class

Large Shareholdings Proposal

This Proposal first appeared in 1985 and has been amended since, but the implementation date is still set for 1 January 1991. France and the UK have stricter rules than those imposed by the Proposal. Under the Proposal a shareholder, in this case the ultimate holder and *not* the nominee, has to inform the company and the relevant regulatory authority within seven days if the holding crosses the 10, 20, 33.3, 50 or 60 per cent thresholds.

The main problem will be enforcement. In the UK shares are registered but in France and West Germany they are bearer securities electronically transferred through Sicovam and Kassenverein. This has also caused some irritation in West Germany where the large universal banks will for the first time have to disclose for whom they are acting as nominees.

Undertaking for collective investments in transferable securities (UCITS)

The UCITS Directive has far-reaching implications not just for investors and fund managers but also for the movement of capital around the Community. There are also substantial tax implications, particularly for countries such as France. It covers all those securities, such as unit trusts, which are designed to spread risk by issuing units which can be bought or redeemed out of the assets of the UCITS.

The Directive first appeared in 1985 and minor amendments for some kinds of investment policies were made in 1988. The Directive is to be implemented by October 1989. It creates a basis whereby an open-ended fund or unit trust that has been approved in one state and meets the Directive's criteria can be sold anywhere in the Community without further permission being sought. However, if a fund is quoted, its quote must not move more than 5 per cent out of line with its net asset value, which must be published at least twice a month.

The following are the essential features governing the regulation, management and operation of the UCITS:

- The UCITS must be authorised and accepted in the home country. Those authorities must approve of the management, the rules of the proposed fund and the choice of depository.

- Managers are restricted to managing the trust

- Depositories have to be liable for their own failures

The following stipulations have been proposed with regard to investment policy. A UCITS

- May include only those securities listed on regular Community exchanges or Community over-the-counter markets

- May invest up to 10 per cent in other instruments but no more than 10 per cent of that in debt instruments

- May not invest in precious metals or precious-metal certificates

- May not invest more than 5 per cent (with certain exceptions) in the securities of any one company

- Must advertise the fact that it is investing more than 35 per cent of its assets

- May not double charge its fees for interconnected UCITS

- May not buy more than 10 per cent of non-voting shares in any one company

Insider dealing

In the wake of the insider dealing scandals that have rocked many of the major financial centres, the Commission put forward a Proposal to harmonise rules to prevent this going on in the Community. When the Proposal was published only the UK, France and Denmark had punitive laws prohibiting insider dealing. West Germany had a voluntary code, but no sanctions; Belgium, the Republic of Ireland and the Netherlands are in the process of complying with the Proposal.

The Proposal defines both a primary and secondary insider and includes what it calls a 'tippee', someone who does not have a direct commercial relation with the company concerned but to whom information is passed. The Proposal outlines the nature of that information; it must be:

- Unpublished

- Quite specific

- Related to one or more issuers of securities

- Of such a nature as to have a material effect on the price of the security

Liberalisation of capital movements

A single market can work only if there is a free flow of capital. The purpose of the Capital Movements Directive (88)361 is to remove all forms of exchange controls, although there are built-in safeguards to prevent short-term instability, that is, where 'exceptional' short-term capital movements might seriously undermine a member state's monetary and exchange-rate policies. The liberalisation of capital movements is discussed further in Chapter 2.

The Capital Movements Directive, adopted by the Council in June 1988, implements Article 67 of the Treaty of Rome and extends original attempts to free up long-term capital transactions. In 1986 the movement of trade credits, listed and unlisted securities and investment funds had been freed up. It obliges member states to:

- Abolish restrictions on movement of capital between members

- Ensure capital transfers are carried out in accordance with the exchange rate at the time of the transaction

- Inform the Commission of certain measures to regulate bank liquidity

- Inform the Commission if protective measures have to be taken to restrict certain capital movements (they may only be applied for up to six months)

When this Directive was introduced only the UK and West Germany had removed all impediments to the movement of capital. At that time the Netherlands was allowing the free outflow of up to Fl 5,000; Spain Pta 50,000; Belgium and Luxembourg BFr 100,000; the Republic of Ireland IR£100 (for non-travel); and Greece allowed private payments of 2,500 ecu a year.

This is an area where there will be extensions. Greece and Portugal are making progress but the Council of Ministers has made provision for a possible extension to 1995 to prevent a sudden damaging effect on these historically heavily protected economies.

Included in the process of liberalising capital flows is allowing free transactions in UCITS (see above) to be implemented by 1 October 1989.

Home/host country control

The concept of home or host country control was established in the First Banking Directive, adopted in December 1977. All twelve member

Mutual recognition

states, as host countries, have to ask the branches of foreign banks to comply with host country rules. The Greek authorities have been allowed until 15 December 1989 to comply. For this host control approach to work there has to be a 'mutual recognition' by national supervisory authorities of legislation and controls operated by other member states.

Under the principle of home country control, enshrined in the Second Banking Directive, a bank or credit institution allowed to perform at home any of the so-called core banking activities by its own regulatory authority will be allowed to do the same throughout the Community without having to establish in member states. The idea is that the home country authority will have overall responsibility for the supervision of the institution, while the host country authorities will regulate the market place. The Directive envisages continuous exchanges of information between regulatory authorities, particularly where an institution is not complying with either home or host regulations.

Under Article 19, the host state also has powers under the notion of 'public good' to insist on quarterly reports and a correction of any non-compliance. It may also take steps to prevent further transactions where non-compliance persists. There are also emergency measures, which are subject to judicial review, available to the host authorities to protect depositors and investors.

Strategic options facing banks

Corporate strategies

A big danger said to face banks in the Community in the run up to 1992 and beyond is the threat of takeover. This could be the fate for some of the plethora of smaller banks and indeed for savings banks. Most of this activity is expected to occur in the UK, Spain, Italy, West Germany and perhaps Luxembourg.

Most banking institutions looking to take advantage of the single market are planning mergers or at least co-operation agreements. Most have accepted the need for on-the-ground expertise, with the UK and German banks in the forefront of forging links with Italian, Spanish and French banks. Others have agreed to reciprocal equity stakes in what must be the advent of a new version of the consortium bank. Some could be construed as 'poison pills', although this is probably not true of the agreement between AMRO and Générale Bank (see p. 138). This deal in itself gives rise to a framework which could bring together even more Community banks under the same umbrella.

The cost of setting up anything other than a wholesale banking operation in another member state is probably prohibitive. There are additional hurdles such as those raised by the Basel Committee's standards laid down for capital adequacy, which includes the stipulation that the 'goodwill' element of any purchase must be deducted from core capital. This leaves only those banks with ample capital as potential buyers of other major banks. The field is even more limited in countries such as Italy, and perhaps to a lesser extent France and West Germany, where many banks are owned by federal or provincial governments or are co-operative associations. Moreover, any attempt to acquire even privately owned banks stirs up all sorts of nationalistic feelings and precipitates battles for control. Often the end result is that the final purchase price exceeds, sometimes substantially, the bank's book value.

Nevertheless, the potential is there. An analysis in the London-based monthly magazine *The Banker* shows that of the 162 Community banks in the world's top 500 (ranked by asset size), thirty-nine are potential acquisition targets. Of the rest, ninety-three cannot be acquired for reasons already stated, while about thirty are simply too big or too important nationally. Of the potential acquisition targets, some twelve are either merchant banks or specialist institutions with limited networks and at least ten of these are controlled by other institutions. It is not necessary to be big to be beautiful in post-1992 Europe but it will be necessary to have friends.

1992 and insurance

UK insurers, with their substantial and sophisticated experience in the insurance industry, should be well placed to take maximum advantage of the single market. UK insurance is among the top five national markets in the Community and as an industry it has been particularly successful in selling policies abroad.

The legislative framework for insurance in the Community will be made up of directives on:

- Direct, non-life insurance (adopted by the Council of Ministers on 2 June 1988)
- Life insurance (still to be tabled)
- Motor liability insurance (still to be tabled)
- Annual and consolidated accounts of insurance companies (Proposal)

- Laws and regulations for the compulsory winding up of insurance companies (Proposal)

- Laws, regulations and administration of insurance contracts (amended Proposal with the Council of Ministers before going to the European Parliament)

- Laws and regulations concerning legal expenses insurance (Council Directive adopted 22 June 1987; implementation by 1 January 1990)

- Credit insurance and suretyship insurance (Council Directive adopted on 22 January 1987; implementation by 1 January 1990)

Legislation on insurance for 1992 is essentially an extension of a body of Community legislation already in existence, which co-ordinates national laws on the establishment and operation of insurance companies. But, despite the presence of co-ordinating and supervisory law, there remain several obstacles to the freedom of an insurance company established in one member state but wanting to cover risks in a fellow member state.

The intention is to get rid of these obstacles in line with those principles governing other aspects of the financial services by, for example:

- Harmonising supervision

- Mutual recognition of other member state controls

- Accepting home country control except in certain specified cases affecting consumer protection

The legislation will distinguish between what it calls mass risk (concerning individuals) and large risk (applicable to firms). This distinction will be further determined by the value of insurance cover.

Consumer protection
It has been accepted that some measure of host country control must be retained because national supervision and control is particularly important for consumer protection in mass risk business.

The cross-selling of insurance between member states is proving a hard nut to crack for the Commission. The Commission has Council approval for a directive allowing the cross-border writing of large commercial non-life cover. The question of 'mass risk' for individuals is still being thrashed out although it is likely that the Council will approve some limited measure for individual cross-border life insurance where it is sought on the individual's 'own initiative'. A major hurdle (as with so many other aspects of financial services legislation) exists in the widely different tax treatment of life insurance by member states.

Appendix 3: Contact addresses

1. World Aid Section
   Room 042
   Department of Trade and Industry
   1–19 Victoria Street
   London SW1H OET
   Tel: 01 215 7877

   This is the central contact point for general information about EC
   Structural Funds, and for information about specific programme
   and project opportunities.

2. European Social Fund Unit
   Department of Employment
   The Civil Service College
   11 Belgrave Road
   London SW1V 1RB
   Tel: 01 834 6644

3. For European Regional Development matters, contact:
   Investment, Development & Accountancy Services Division
   Department of Trade and Industry
   Room 229
   66–74 Victoria Street
   London SW1E 6SW
   Tel: 01 215 7877

4. For FEOGA guidance, contact:
   Ministry of Agriculture, Fisheries and Food
   EC Division ECII
   10 Whitehall Place
   London SW1A 2HH
   Tel: 01 270 3000

5. Office of the UK Permanent Representative to the EC
   6 Rond Point Schuman
   1040 Brussels
   Tel: Brussels 010 322 230 6205

6. European Coal and Steel Community
   Directorate-General for Credit and Investments
   Bâtiment Jean Monnet
   Kirchberg
   Luxembourg
   Tel: 010 352 43011/3234

7. Liaison Office for the UK
   European Investment Bank
   68 Pall Mall
   London SW1Y 5ES
   Tel: 01 839 3351

In addition, leading UK banks are a good source of information on EC finance.

Bibliography

General

Adrian Buckley, *Multinational Finance* (Philip Allan, 1986)

Jack Butler, *The Importer's Handbook* (Woodhead-Faulkner, 1988)

Michael Brett, *How to Read the Financial Pages* (Century Hutchinson, 1987)

Paolo Cecchini, *1992: The European Challenge. The Benefits of the Single Market* (Gower, 1988)

Philip Coggan, *The Money Machine* (Penguin, 1986)

David Cox, *Elements of Banking* (John Murray, 1988)

Daily Telegraph, *How to Export* (Telegraph Publications, 1988)

Department of Trade and Industry, *The Single Market* (DTI, 1988)

Economist Intelligence Unit, *European Trends* (The Economist Publications, 1988)

European Community Official Publications, *The European Commission's Powers of Investigation in Enforcement of Competition Law* (1984)★

— *European Economy: The Economics of 1992* (1988)★

C. J. Higson, *Business Finance* (Butterworths, 1986)

Sydney Paulden, *The Export Times Trade Finance Handbook* (Export Times, 1987)

Derek Ross, Ian Clark, Serajul Taiyeb, *International Treasury Management* (Woodhead-Faulkner, 1987)

John Stapleton, *Elements of Export Marketing* (Woodhead-Faulkner, 1984)

Alasdair Watson, *Finance of International Trade* (Chartered Institute of Bankers, 1985)

Leonard Waxman, *Finance of International Trade* (Graham and Trotman, 1985)

D. P. Whiting, *Finance of Foreign Trade* (Longman, 1985)

★ These publications are available from The Commission of the European Communities, 8 Storey's Gate, London SW1P 3AT.

*National Westminster Bank Publications**

Check List for Documentary Credits
Export Finance and Insurance
Foreign Bonds and Guarantees
Guidance Notes for the Completion of an Application to
 Open a Documentary Letter of Credit
Guide to Exporting and Importing
Guide to the Completion of Money Transfer Forms
Services for the Exporter and Importer
Buyer Finance Available from NatWest
Customer Statement Guide
Expedited Collection Service
Export Ease
An Export Finance House Service
Forfaiting
International Trade Bulletin
Your Currency Account Explained
Banker's Acceptances
Currency Exposure Management
Currency Options
ECUs
Financial Futures
Foreign Exchange for Exporters
Forward Rate Agreements
Interest Rate Exposure Management
Interest Rate Options
Introduction to Currency and Interest Rate Swaps
Official Sources of Finance and Aid in the UK (1989)

* These publications are available through branches of National Westminster Bank.

Glossary

Acceptances *See* bank bills.

Admissions Directive An EC directive which sets minimum standards for company listings on stock exchanges (*see also* Listing Particulars Directive, Interim Reports Directive).

Bank bills Also known as 'acceptances'. These are term bills of exchange that have been accepted by a bank under a 'documentary letter of credit'. The bank undertakes to pay that bill at maturity, which means the company which has drawn the bill can sell it in the discount market to provide immediate finance. Not to be confused with 'clean acceptance credits', which do not use documentary l/cs.

Banker's draft A payment instruction, similar to a cheque, drawn by a bank. It offers more security of payment than a cheque drawn on the importer's own account.

Bill of exchange A bill drawn by a supplying company on a buying company, stating that the buyer will pay the supplier a set amount of money at a set future date. The buyer 'accepts' the debt by signing the face of the bill and sends it back. The supplier can hold on to the bill, waiting until it matures to receive payment, or can sell the bill to someone else, such as a bank or discount house, for a discount, thus receiving cash right away. This latter action is known as 'discounting', and provides the supplier (the 'drawer of the bill') with short-term trade finance.

Capital Movements Directive EC directive to remove all forms of exchange controls within the Community.

Caps, collars and floors Forms of interest-rate options enabling companies to hedge against adverse movements in rates by limiting them from moving above or below certain levels. A cap puts a limit on how high rates can rise; a floor puts a limit on how low they can drop; a collar is a combination of the two, locking interest rates into a specified range.

Cecchini Report *1992: The Benefits of a Single Market*, a book by Paolo Cecchini published in 1988 and funded by the European Commission. It makes an estimate of the costs of a fragmented European market, which it puts at £140 billion, and tries to assess the benefits that will come from the single market.

CHAPS (Clearing House Automated Payments System) An electronic network through which sterling transfers are made between banks. It is a secure and reliable method using automated high-speed computers and ensuring same-day value transfers.

Collection of cheques, bills of exchange and other trade documents The procedure whereby an exporter's bank sends cheques abroad for payment by the foreign bank on which they are drawn, or sends bills of exchange (or other documents where bills are not used) abroad for payment or acceptance by the importer. The bank may lend money to the exporter against collections – these are called 'advances against collection of documents', or 'documentary advances'.

Clean acceptance credit A bill of exchange drawn by a company on a bank, which the bank 'accepts' by signing it. This means the bank accepts to pay the holder at maturity. The bills are then like 'bank bills', and the company which drew them can discount them in the London market, thus raising short-term finance. When the bill matures, and the bank pays the holder, the bank is reimbursed by the company which drew the bill. Clean acceptance credits are a substitute for overdrafts in big company finance, and are referred to as 'clean' to distinguish them from acceptances under documentary letters of credit.

Commercial paper Short-term paper issued by companies and other big borrowers to investors at a discount to its face value.

Correspondent bank A bank in another country through which international payment instructions are transmitted. Cash is rarely physically sent from one country to another. Instead, international funds transfers are made by banks debiting or crediting the accounts that they hold with their correspondent banks around the world.

Cut-off time The time of day a bank in another country will not execute payment orders on the day they are received.

Direct acceptance bid A method by which banks approach large companies to offer, on a one-off basis, lower rates for clean acceptance credits.

Documentary advance A loan to a company based on a percentage of the value of export documents forwarded through a bank to the overseas buyer for collection (i.e. payment).

Documentary letter of credit A written undertaking given by a bank on behalf of the buyer, to pay the seller an amount of money within a specific time, provided the seller presents documents strictly in accordance with the terms laid down in the letter of credit. Apart from an advance payment, this is the most secure method of payment.

Ecu (European Currency Unit) An embryo common currency made up of the weighted average of the individual currencies of member states.

Electronic Data Interchange (EDI) The electronic transfer of information (such as orders, invoices, letters of credit) between trading companies, using computer networks; EDI is gradually taking over from paper-based documentation.

Exchange Rate Mechanism (ERM) The mechanism within the European Monetary System which keeps the exchange rates of participating currencies within a narrow band. The UK is in the EMS, but does not participate in the ERM.

Eurobond A bond denominated in a Eurocurrency and issued in the Euromarkets by a large company, bank, government or supranational institution to raise long-term finance at competitive rates.

Eurocurrency A currency traded outside its country of origin, such as Eurodollars or Eurosterling. Eurocurrency loans are raised in the offshore international financial markets, known as the Eurocurrency markets.

Euromarkets The collective name given to the Eurocurrency and Euroband markets.

Euronote A short- or medium-term form of Eurobond, issued direct to investors in the Euromarkets.

European Agricultural Guidance and Guarantee Fund Usually known by its French acronym FEOGA, this is an EC Structural Fund. The guarantee section controls agricultural markets through a complicated systems of licences, levies and refunds. The much smaller guidance section makes grants to companies marketing and processing agricultural products.

European Central Bank At present, just a concept that could lead to full monetary union within the EC. Its objectives would include maintaining prices at similar levels throughout the Community, managing a common currency, co-ordinating all official foreign exchange and money market intervention on behalf of member states, and being a mouthpiece for the EC at international gatherings.

European Coal and Steel Community (ECSC)   Formed in 1951 to set up and supervise a single market for coal and steel, the ECSC provides finance for modernising the coal and steel industries and for creating new jobs in the areas where these industries are located.

European Investment Bank (EIB)   The institution owned by the twelve member states whose purpose is to raise funds in domestic and international capital markets in order to on-lend, on a non-profit-making basis, to public authorities and companies to help finance the cost of industrial, energy and infrastructure projects.

European Monetary Co-operation Fund   The fund with which EMS members place dollar and gold reserves in exchange for ecu. These reserves are then used to intervene in the foreign exchange markets to maintain currency parities. Often thought of as an embryo European Central Bank.

European Monetary System (EMS)   The system designed to maintain exchange rate stability within the EC (although not all member states are EMS members) and eventually to create the right conditions for a true European currency and full monetary union.

European Regional Development Fund (ERDF)   An EC Structural Fund targeted at poorer regions to help correct disparities of wealth and development within the Community.

European Social Fund (ESF)   An EC Structural Fund for improving job opportunities for workers through training and re-training. Grants are directed at regions and groups of workers hardest hit by unemployment.

Export Credits Guarantee Department (ECGD)   UK government department which insures UK firms against the risk of importers, to whom they have given credit, not paying up. Private sector insurers also provide credit insurance. In addition, ECGD provides 'bankers's guarantees' against which banks will lend to exporters at special rates of interest, knowing that in case of non-payment they can turn to ECGD for reimbursement.

Factoring A form of short-term finance where a bank buys a company's invoices. The bank pre-pays up to 80 per cent of the value of the invoices, and the rest when the company's customer settles the invoice. Factoring also includes 100 per cent bad debt protection to the company, and a sales ledger service.

Forfaiting The purchase from an exporter by a bank of a series of bills of exchange or promissory notes after the goods have been shipped to the importer. It is a form of short- or medium-term finance, similar to factoring, with the key exceptions that forfaiting usually provides 100 per cent finance (factoring is 80 per cent), and it is does not include a sales ledger service.

Forward agreement Also called 'forward/forward', this is a technique used by companies to protect against adverse movements in interest rates. It is an agreement for a company to borrow from, or deposit with, a bank a fixed amount at a fixed rate of interest for a fixed period in the future.

Forward-rate agreement A contract to pay or receive the difference between an agreed rate of interest and the floating LIBOR rate for a forward period. There is no obligation to make a loan or deposit – the agreement is based on a notional sum and covers only the interest rate difference, unlike a forward agreement where a real sum is involved.

Forward exchange contract A currency hedging device, where a company makes a binding agreement with a bank to switch one currency for another at a specific future date (or within a range of dates) and at a set rate.

Franchising The system by which one business allows others to use its product, services or system, and the business name and image, to repeat its success in other areas, in return for a fee and a percentage of the new business generated.

Futures Financial instruments giving the buyer the right to buy a financial commitment or commodity in the future. In trade finance, currency futures and interest-rate futures can be used for hedging against unfavourable fluctuations in exchange rates and interest rates. A currency future performs the same function as a forward exchange contract; the difference is that futures can only be bought on exchanges, and not over-the-counter from banks.

Hedging The technique whereby companies lock their future foreign currency receivables or payables into a set rate against sterling. They therefore hedge against the risk of adverse exchange-rate movement.

Home country control   A principle enshrined in the EC's Second Banking Directive whereby a bank or credit institution which is allowed to carry out at 'home' any of the core banking activities by its own regulatory authority will be allowed to do the same in all other member states – the 'host' countries. However, each host country will have certain supervisory duties and reserve powers.

Interbank transfer of funds   The most common method of making international payments; it offers greater speed and security than cheque or drafts. The transfers take place through the SWIFT or CHAPS networks.

Interim Reports Directive   An EC directive which sets the minimum standards stock-exchange-listed companies must follow for interim (first six months) reports (*see also* Admissions Directive, Listing Particulars Directive).

Investment Services Directive   The central piece of legislation governing how investment services firms will operate after 1992. This will include minimum authorisation standards concerning capital adequacy requirements, investor compensation and client money segregation.

LIBID (London Interbank Bid Rate)   The interest rate at which one bank will borrow from another in the London money markets.

LIBOR (London Interbank Offered Rate)   The interest rate at which one bank will lend to another in the London money markets. Banks often lend to large corporate customers at rates just above LIBOR.

Limited recourse finance   Finance for a project wholly or partly on the credit of the project itself, with the revenue from the completed project being the sole or primary source of repayment. Also known as project finance.

Listing Particulars Directive   An EC directive which sets out the standards to be followed by companies providing information to stock exchanges (*see also* Admissions Directive, Interim Reports Directive).

Management buy-out (MBO)   The process whereby a group of managers in a large company buy a part (sometimes all) of it with the help of outside equity and loans.

Medium-term note (MTN)   A form of paper issued by companies to investors in order to raise medium-term finance. Similar to commercial paper but longer-dated.

Office banking Electronic banking system whereby corporate treasurers can initiate money transfers and communicate in other ways with their bank using a computer terminal in their office.

Open account The method of payment whereby the seller sends the goods and documents to the buyer, with no safeguards against non-payment. The seller relies on the honesty and integrity of the buyer to pay on time.

Options Financial instruments which give the buyer the right, but not the obligation, to buy or sell a financial commitment or commodity at a set price. In the context of trade finance, currency options and interest-rate options are useful hedging tools. Options can be bought over-the-counter from a bank, or they can be traded on exchanges.

Negotiation of cheques and bills of exchange The procedure whereby an exporter can get an advance on an uncleared foreign cheque or on a sight bill of exchange by asking the bank to negotiate – that is, purchase – the cheque or bill at the time they are sent for collection. If the cheque or bill remains unpaid, the bank has recourse to the exporter for the full amount.

Second Banking Directive This lays down the rules under which banks and related credit institutions will operate after 1992. These rules include a minimum capital base below which a bank cannot fall; the principle of 'home country' control as the basis for the regulation of banks offering services across the EC; and definitions of what types of business a bank may do.

Single European Act The 1987 Act which declared that most of the EC Directives which have as their objective the creation of a single market could be passed by a majority vote of the Council of Ministers, instead of a unanimous one; 31 December 1992 was set as the final date for establishing the internal market.

Spot rate The current rate at which one currency can be exchanged for another.

Swaps An interest-rate swap is where two borrowers of different currencies agree to swap the interest payments on their loans. A currency swap is where the two borrowers agree to swap the capital they each have to repay.

SWIFT (Society for Worldwide Interbank Financial Telecommunications) An international electronic network through which banks transfer funds between one another. There are two main types of transfer: urgent and standard. Interbank transfers are quicker and safer than cheques or drafts.

Syndicated loan   A medium- or long-term loan raised in the Euromarkets by a syndicate of banks under a lead manager. The interest rate is linked to LIBOR.

UCITS (Undertaking for Collective Investments in Transferable Securities) Directive   An EC directive which allows securities such as unit trusts to be sold anywhere in the EC, provided they have been approved in one state and they meet the Directive's criteria.

Venture capital   Equity and/or loans provided by financial institutions to growing unquoted companies to allow them to grow further. Most venture capital funds are linked to banks, insurance companies and pension funds. Venture capital is also used in management buy-outs.

Index

acceptance credit, 44, 62, 66, 161
  see also clean acceptance credit
acceptances, 161
acquisitions, 3, 111, 112, 123, 128, 129, 131, 144, 149
Agnelli, 114
Air France, 96
Alcoa, 126
Algemene Bank Nederland, 138
Allianz, 113
Allied Irish Banks, 140
American International Group (AIG), 44
amortising repayment, 67
Amsterdam–Rotterdam Bank (AMRO), 5, 138, 153
Anderson, Keith, 124
anti-competitive practices, 13
Ashford International Hotel, 128
associated banks, 140
Association of British Factors, 53–4

B&W Loudspeakers, 51, 123, 124–5
Bairstow, John, 128
Banca d'America & d'Italia, 5
Banco Comercial Transatlantico, 5
Banco de Bilbao, 5
Banco de Vizcaya, 5
Banco Santander, 5
Bank of England, 8, 22
Bank of Ireland, 140
Bank of Italy, 137
Bank of Spain, 141
Banker, The, 154

banks, 2, 3, 4–6, 7, 8, 9, 13, 29, 36, 56, 58, 66, 67, 68, 71, 76, 78, 79, 81, 87, 88, 93–4, 97, 109, 111, 121–2, 123, 154, 162, 163, 164–5, 166, 167, 168
accounts of banks, 145–6
bank bills, 136, 161, 162
banker's drafts, 29, 30–31, 43, 44, 144, 161, 166, 168
banker's guarantees, 49–51, 164
branch accounts, 145
branches, 147, 153
cheques, 29–30, 144, 161, 162, 166, 167, 168
concealed reserves, 146
electronic transfers, 2, 29, 31–4, 147, 167
forward positions, 146
loans, 10, 61, 62, 65, 70, 140
overdrafts, 5, 37, 38, 52, 119, 136, 137, 138, 139, 140, 141, 142, 162
trading securities portfolios, 146
  see also particular types of banks (associated banks; commercial banks; deposit banks; merchant banks; savings banks, etc.); *and also* under specialised topics (forfaiting; interbank transfer of funds; office banking, etc.); and under individual countries (Belgium; Denmark; France; Greece; Italy; Japan; Luxembourg; Netherlands, The; Portugal; Republic of Ireland; Spain; UK; USA; West Germany)

Banque de France, 136
Banque Générale du Luxembourg, 138
Banque Internationale à Luxembourg, 138
Barcelona Olympics, 104
Basel Committee, 143, 154
Basic Research in Industrial Technologies for Europe (BRITE), 109
Bayswater Tubes and Sections Limited, 54, 123, 126–7
bearer securities, 150
Belgium
  banking system, 133–4
  banks, 5, 10, 133, 134
  capital movements, 152
  insider dealing, 151
Belgo-Luxembourg Exchange Institute, 133
bills of exchange, 2, 39, 54, 56, 62, 126, 161, 162, 165, 167
BP, 64
  Forties Field, 94
British Aerospace, 96
British Coal, 36, 116
British Franchise Association (BFA), 99, 100–101
British Vita PLC, 123, 130–31
Broadgate office development, 91
brokerages, 12, 14, 148
brokers, 47
building societies, 140, 144
bullet repayment, 65, 67, 68
Bundesbank, 24, 142
Bureau of European Consumer Organisations, 20
Business Expansion Scheme, 116, 129
Business Improvement Services Scheme, 107
business stategy, 1, 2, 65, 122

buy-outs, 3
  see also leveraged buy-outs
    (LBOs); management buy-
    outs (MBOs)

Caisse d'Épargne de l'État, 138
Caixa Geral de Depositos, 139
capital allowances, 96
capital funds, 3, 11–22
capital movements, 11, 150
  liberalisation of, 21–2, 152
  see also Belgium; EC; Greece;
    Italy; Luxembourg;
    Netherlands, The;
    Portugal; Spain; UK; West
    Germany
caps, 78, 79, 81, 161
  see also collars; floors
Cecchini Report, 9, 10, 13–17,
    162
Channel Tunnel, 128
  see also Eurotunnel
CHAPS (Clearing House
    Automated Payments
    System), 4, 31, 32–3, 162,
    166
clean acceptance credit, 161,
    162
clean/documentary collection,
    39–40, 162
clearing banks, 4, 100, 101, 102,
    133, 138
collars, 78, 81–3, 161
  see also caps; floors
Commercial Bank of Greece,
    136
commercial banks, 134, 136,
    138, 139, 141
commercial paper, 63–4, 66, 67,
    72, 149, 162
  see also Eurocommercial
    Paper (ECP); USA
Commerzbank, 6, 141
Common Agricultural Policy,
    107
  see also European Agricultural
    Guidance and Guarantee
    Fund (FEOGA)
Compagnie du Midi, 113
Companies House, 145
competition, 3, 5, 14, 17, 18,
    71, 109, 135, 136, 147

competition – continued
  see also anti-competitive
    practices; Japan; USA
computer revolution, 59
consortium banks, 153
consumer credit, 144
consumer protection, 9, 155
convertible bonds, 121–2
convertible loan stock, 73
co-operative agreements, 153
co-operative and investment
    banking, 6
co-operative associations, 154
co-operative takeovers, 113
Cornhill Insurance, 113
corporate advisory services,
    111–12
correspondent banks, 162
Costains, 104
Council of Ministers, 11, 147,
    152, 154, 155, 167
credit, 17, 18, 37, 67, 70, 71,
    126, 133, 147, 164, 166
  see also acceptance credit;
    clean acceptance credit;
    consumer credit; customer
    credit; deferred payment
    credit; documentary letters
    of credit; UK
credit-checking agencies, 59
credit controls, 136
credit institutions, 147, 153,
    166, 167
  see also mortgage credit
    institutions
credit insurance, 44–8, 49, 155,
    164
Crédit Lyonnais, 6
credit ratings, 121
credit reference, 2, 36, 58–9, 144
currency exposure management,
    2, 85–8
currency loans, 231
currency options, 87–8
customer credit, 38, 52, 54
customer services, 148
cut-off time, 162

Danmarks Nationalbank, 135
Dartford River Crossing, 91
de Bary, H. Alfred, 5
De Benedetti, 114

debentures, 73
debt securities, 149
deferred payment credit, 44,
    55
De Nederlandsche Bank,
    139
Denmark
  banking system, 134–5
  deposit guarantee, 146
  insider dealing, 151
deposit banks, 135
deposit guarantee schemes, 139,
    141, 146–7
  see also Denmark; Greece;
    Republic of Ireland
Deutsche Bank, 4, 131, 141
Direct Acceptance Bid (DAB),
    62
discounting, 136, 161
  see also invoice discounting
documentary advance, 163
documentary letters of credit, 2,
    18, 34, 38, 40–43, 161, 162,
    163
Dresdner Bank, 141

EC
  Directives: Admissions
    Directive, 148–9, 161, 166;
    Branch Accounts Directive,
    146; Capital Adequacy
    Directive, 147; Capital
    Movements Directive, 20,
    21, 152, 161; Consolidated
    Supervision Directive, 136;
    First Banking Directive, 7,
    143, 152; Interim Reports
    Directive, 149, 161, 166;
    Investment Services
    Directive, 10, 11, 147, 148,
    166; Listing Particulars
    Directive, 149, 161, 166;
    Mortgage Credit Directive,
    145; Second Banking
    Directive, 5, 7, 8, 10, 11,
    134, 143–4, 145, 147, 148,
    153, 166, 167; Solvency
    Ratio Directive, 143;
    UCITS Directive, 150–51,
    152, 168
  environment programme, 109
  loans and grants, 91, 103–9

EC – *continued*
proposals: Large
Shareholdings Proposal,
150; Own Funds Proposal,
143; Prospectus Proposal,
149; Single Banking
Licence, 5
ecu (European Currency Unit),
19, 20, 23, 24–6, 87, 163,
164
EFTPOS, 144, 147
Electronic Data Interchange
(EDI), 2, 4, 34–6, 144, 163
employee issues, 149
ENI, 114
Equipment Leasing Association,
96
equipment, standardisation of,
12
equity, 4, 72, 111–15, 117–18,
121, 153, 166, 168
and law, 113
see also France; Italy;
Portugal; Spain;
Switzerland; UK; West
Germany
Eurobonds, 26, 70, 73, 111,
120–22, 149, 163
Eurocommercial Paper (ECP),
64
Eurocurrency 120, 121, 163
Eurocurrency loans, 63, 163
Eurodollars, 120, 163
Euromarkets, 70–71, 120, 121,
122, 163, 168
Euronotes, 70, 71–2, 121
European Agricultural Guidance
and Guarantee Fund
(FEOGA), 104, 107,
164
European Central Bank, 7, 20,
27–8, 163, 164
European Coal and Steel
Community (ECSC), 104,
108, 164
European Community
Banking Federation, 8
non-G10 Community
members, 9
European Council, 104
European Franchise Federation,
101

European Investment Bank
(EIB), 104, 108–9, 164
European League for Economic
Co-operation, 24
European Monetary Co-
operation Fund, 23, 27,
164
European Monetary System
(EMS), 19, 20, 22–4, 140,
163, 164
European Parliament, 155
European Regional
Development Fund
(ERDF), 104, 105, 107, 164
European Research Co-
ordination Agency
(EUREKA), 109
European Social Fund (ESF),
104, 105, 164
European Strategic Programme
for Research &
Development in
Information Technologies
(ESPRIT), 109
European Venture Capital
Association (EVCA), 117
Eurosterling, 120, 121, 122, 163
Eurotunnel, 91
exchange controls, 5, 19, 21,
152, 161
see also France; Italy
exchange rate mechanism
(ERM), 22, 23–4, 25, 163
exchange rates, 7, 19, 20, 21,
22, 30, 75, 148, 163, 165,
166
Expo '92, 104

factoring, 2, 51–4, 124, 125,
144, 164–5
Fiat, 3
fixed-rate finance, 65, 165
fixed-term loans, 66, 68, 69, 70,
139
floating rates, 65, 73, 75, 78, 81,
90
floors, 78, 79, 81, 161
see also caps; collars; interest-
rate floor agreement
foreign bond issue, 73
foreign currency account, 85–6
foreign exchange 144, 163

foreign exchange contracts, 86–7
forfaiting, 54–8, 123, 126, 144,
165
forward agreement, 165
forward-exchange contract, 165
forward positions, 146
forward-rate agreement, 75–7,
78, 165
France
banking system, 135–6
banks, 5–6, 10, 120, 153, 154
companies, 104, 116, 117
equity, 113, 114
exchange controls, 5, 21
insider dealing, 151
leasing, 95–6, 97
shares, 150
tax collection system, 8, 150
venture capital, 116, 117
franchising, 2, 91, 99–102
see also UK; USA
free issues, 149
futures, 88, 144, 148, 165
see also interest-rate futures

Gardini, 114
Générale Bank, 5, 138, 153
goodwill, 154
government securities, 148, 149
Greece
banking system, 133, 136
capital movements, 152
deposit guarantee, 146
home/host country control,
153
structural funding, 104–5,
106
Guinness, 36, 114

hedging, 161, 165–6, 167
Hellenic Industrial
Development Bank, 136
Hessische Landesbank, 5
holiday companies, 88
Holiday Inn, 128
home/host country control, 8, 9,
11, 13, 152–3, 155, 166,
167
see also Greece
hostile takeovers, 3, 4

IBM, 35

ICI, 36
inflation, 21, 24
information sources on EC
    finance, 2, 103–9
information technologies, 36,
    109
INS-GE information services,
    35
insider dealing, 151
    see also Belgium; Denmark;
        France; Netherlands, The;
        Republic of Ireland; UK;
        West Germany
insider trading, 11, 148
insurance, 11, 12, 14, 17, 18,
    49, 154–5
    see also credit insurance; legal
        expenses insurance; life
        insurance; motor liability
        insurance; suretyship
        insurance; UK
insurance companies, 12,
    113–14, 154, 155, 168
Insurance Services Group, 47
Interbank transfer of funds, 29,
    31–4, 166, 168
    see also CHAPS; SWIFT
interest-rate floor agreement, 79
interest-rate futures, 77
interest-rate options, 77–80,
    161, 167
    see also USA
interest-rate swaps, 83, 89–90,
    167
interest rates, 7, 18, 36, 62, 63,
    65, 67, 68, 75, 76, 81, 136,
    138, 142, 148, 161, 164,
    165, 166, 168
    see also floating rates
interest-rate risk management,
    2, 75–83
International Chamber of
    Commerce, 42
International Stock Exchange,
    63
investment banks, 3, 72, 135,
    136, 139, 141
    see also European Investment
        Bank (EIB)
investment services, 143
Investors Overseas Services, 114
invoice discounting, 52–4

IRI, 114
ISTEL, 35
Italy
    banking, 136–7
    banks, 153, 154
    companies, 114, 117
    equity, 113, 114
    exchange controls, 21
    joint ventures, 3
    venture capital, 117

Japan
    banks, 10, 33, 120
    competition, 1, 109
joint ventures, 1, 3, 112, 139
    see also Italy

Kassenverein, 150
Kirkup, William and Peter,
    126
Kredietbank Luxembourgeoise,
    138

Laing, 104
large exposures, 146
leasing, 3, 91, 95–7, 144
    see also France; UK; USA;
        West Germany
legal expenses insurance, 155
level playing-field, 4
leveraged buy-outs (LBOs), 71,
    130
LIBID (London Interbank Bid
    Rate), 166
LIBOR (London Interbank
    Offered Rate), 61, 62, 63,
    65, 66, 68, 70, 76, 78, 79,
    90, 165, 166, 168
life insurance, 155
limited recourse financing, 2,
    91–4, 166
    see also project finance
listed companies, 11, 112, 148,
    149, 161
Lloyds, 131
loans *see* banks; *and also* under
    specialised topics (currency
    loans; Eurocurrency loans;
    fixed-term loan schemes;
    long-term borrowing;
    medium-term borrowing;
    syndicated loans; etc.)

local authority debt securities,
    149
London International Financial
    Futures Exchange
    (LIFFE), 77, 88
long-term borrowing, 2, 65, 67,
    73, 91, 135, 137, 139, 141,
    142, 168
Luxembourg
    banking system, 137–8
    banks, 153
    capital movements, 152
    tax haven, 8
    withholding tax, 7–8

management buy-outs (MBOs),
    120, 166, 168
Marcus, Martin, 128
market line, 62–3
medium-term borrowing, 2, 65,
    66, 67, 68, 69, 70, 91, 123,
    137, 139, 142, 165, 167, 168
medium-term notes (MTNs),
    72, 166–7
    see also USA
merchant banks, 5, 12
mergers, 3, 5, 112, 140, 144,
    149, 153
Mitterrand, François, 5
Moët Hennessy, 114
mortgage credit institutions,
    135, 141, 143, 144–5
mortgages, 6, 10, 135, 141, 144
motor liability insurance, 154
multinationals, 2
multiple option facility (MOF),
    66, 68, 69, 73
mutual recognition, 8, 9, 153,
    155

National Bank of Greece, 136
negotiation of cheques, 167
    see also banks
Netherlands, The
    banking system, 138–9
    banks, 5
    capital movements, 152
    insider dealing, 151
new technologies, 12
Next, 64
North Sea, 91, 94
Northern Bank, 140

one-stop banking, 133
open account, 167
options, 148, 153–4, 167
    see also currency options;
        interest-rate options;
        multiple option facility
over-the-counter markets, 151,
    165, 167
Own Funds, 143

P&O, 36
Padoa Schioppa report, 22
PanFinancial, 44, 46
partnerships, 5, 111, 116–17,
    137
pensions, 114, 168
'poison pills', 3, 153
portfolio management, 144, 148
Portugal
    banking system, 139
    banks, 5
    capital movements, 152
    equity, 114–15
    structural funding, 104, 105
Post Office Savings Bank, 140
Post Office Savings System, 139
Postbank, 138
Price Waterhouse, 9
pricing, 9–10, 13, 64, 79
project finance, 166
promissory notes, 54, 55, 56,
    58, 63, 165
prospectuses, 148
    see also EC
public offers, 11, 149
publishing, 149

Queens Moat Houses PLC,
    128–9

Rabobanks, 138
reciprocity, 10, 153
repayment holiday, 65, 67, 68
Republic of Ireland
    banking system, 139–40
    capital movements, 152
    deposit guarantee, 146
    insider dealing, 151
    structural funding, 104, 105
research and development, 109

revolving underwriting facility
    (RUF), 73
rights issue, 129
Rothmans, 36
Royal Bank of Scotland, 5

safety standards, harmonisation
    of, 3
Sainsbury, 34, 64
savings banks, 135, 138, 139,
    140, 141, 153
securities, 11, 12, 70, 109, 144,
    147–8, 149, 151, 152, 168
    see also bearer securities;
        government securities; local
        authority debt securities;
        trading securities;
        transferable securities
securities transaction taxes, 11,
    149
Sellers, Rod, 130
share-swaps, 3
shares, shareholdings, 6, 11, 73,
    119, 144, 148, 150, 151
    see also EC; France; UK;
        West Germany
short-term borrowing, 2, 61–4,
    65, 91, 135, 136, 137, 138,
    139, 140, 141, 142, 162,
    165
Sicovam, 150
Siemens, 4
Simplification of International
    Trade Procedures Board
    (SITPRO), 42
Single European Act, 1, 167
Single European currency, 7,
    19, 20
    see also ecu; European
        Monetary System (EMS)
single market, 1, 3, 4, 7, 20, 21,
    46, 112, 125, 153, 162, 164,
    167
sovereignty, 7–8
Spain
    banking system, 140–41
    banks, 5, 153
    capital movements, 152
    equity, 113, 114–15
    venture capital, 116, 117
specialist banks, 141
spot rates, 85, 86, 87, 167

stock exchange listings, 11, 111,
    161
stock exchanges, 6, 148, 149
    see also International Stock
        Exchange; UK
stockbroking, 141
Structural Funds, 104, 164
    see also Greece; Portugal;
        Republic of Ireland
suretyship insurance, 155
swaps, 167
    see also interest-rate swaps;
        share swaps
SWIFT (Society for Worldwide
    Interbank Financial
    Telecommunications), 4,
    31, 33, 34, 166, 167–8
Switzerland, 137
    equity, 115
syndicate of banks, 70, 73, 112,
    121
syndicated loans, 70–71, 168

takeovers, 3, 4, 77, 140, 153
    see also co-operative
        takeovers; hostile
        takeovers; UK; USA
taxation, 148, 150
    harmonisation, 7, 8
    see also securities transaction
        taxes; withholding tax; *and
        also* under individual
        countries, France;
        Luxembourg; UK; West
        Germany
technical standards,
    harmonisation of, 3
tender-to-contract cover, 87–8
Times, The
    Top 100 companies, 36
Trade Indemnity (TI), 44, 46,
    47
trade references, 58–9
trading securities, 146
Trafalgar House, 36, 104
transferable securities, 148,
    150
Treaty of Rome
    Article 67, 152
    Article 85, 12, 13
    Article 86, 12
Trustee Savings Bank, 140

UK
  banking system, 133
  banks, 4–5, 8, 10, 18, 22, 32,
    33, 36, 40–41, 43, 55, 58,
    71, 85, 86, 91, 95, 101, 104,
    120, 123, 124–5, 126, 129,
    131, 133, 138, 139–40, 153
  capital movements, 152
  companies, 36, 103–4, 105,
    107, 108, 109, 113–14, 115,
    116, 117–18, 120, 121–31
  Department of Trade and
    Industry (DTI), 104, 105,
    107, 108
  equity, 113, 117–18
  and the European Monetary
    System, 1, 23–4, 163
  Export Credits Guarantee
    Department (ECGD), 38,
    40, 44, 46, 47, 48, 50, 51,
    164
  franchising, 99, 100–101
  insider dealing, 151
  insurance, 154
  leasing, 95–6, 97
  Queen's Award for Export
    Achievement, 124

UK – *continued*
  shares, 150
  Stock Market, 130
  takeovers, 3
  venture capital, 116, 117–18,
    120
  withholding tax, 7
Ulster Bank, 140
underwriting, 47, 68, 71, 72,
    119, 122, 148
  see also revolving
    underwriting facility (RUF)
unit trusts, 150
Unlisted Securities Market, 63,
    130
universal banks, 141, 150
USA
  banks, 10, 89, 120, 134
  commercial paper, 63, 72
  competition, 1, 20, 109
  franchising, 99
  interest-rate options,
    78
  leasing, 97
  medium-term notes, 72
  takeovers, 71
  venture capital, 115, 120

venture capital, 3, 111, 115–19,
    168
  see also European Venture
    Capital Association
    (EVCA); *see also* under
    individual countries,
    France; Italy; Spain; UK;
    USA; West Germany
Venture Consort Scheme, 117

warrants, 149
West Germany
  banking system, 133, 141–2
  banks, 4, 5, 6, 10, 24, 32, 43,
    131, 153, 154
  capital movements, 152
  companies, 104, 117, 141, 142
  equity, 113–14
  insider dealing, 151
  leasing, 95–6
  shares, 150
  venture capital, 116, 117
  withholding tax, 8
Westdeutsche Landesbank, 5
withholding tax, 7–8
  see also Luxembourg; UK;
    West Germany